D0914228

# THE SELF, SUPERVENIENCE AND PERSONAL IDENTITY

# The Self, Supervenience and Personal Identity

RONALD G. ALEXANDER

## Ashgate

Aldershot • Brookfield USA • Singapore • Sydney

© R. Alexander 1997

Published by
Ashgate Publishing Limited
Gower House
Croft Road
Aldershot
Hants GU11 3HR
England

Ashgate Publishing Company
Old Post Road
Brookfield
Vermont 05036
USA

BD
438.5
.A44
1997

**British Library Cataloguing in Publication Data**
Alexander, Ronald
 The self, supervenience and personal identity. - (Avebury
 series in philosophy)
 1.Self (Philosophy)
 I.Title
 126

**Library of Congress Catalog Card Number:** 97-73210

ISBN 1 85972 603 8

Printed and bound by Athenaeum Press, Ltd.,
Gateshead, Tyne & Wear.

# Contents

# Acknowledgements

Professor Panayot Butchvarov of the University of Iowa was extremely helpful in bringing this project to completion. His analytic acumen and encouragement were much appreciated. The reader will notice that I engage him in a "dialogue" in Chapter Four. However, one should not assume that he agrees with my position on the issue of tropes (or on other topics for that matter) even though his analysis of 'generic properties' was very helpful in my coming to the conclusion that the self is a trope.

I also want to thank Laird Addis, James Duerlinger, Richard Fumerton, and Alan Nagel for their helpful critiques. Greg Scholtz expertly advised me in respect to stylistic matters, and any problem that remains is my responsibility.

# Preface

Many philosophers have written on the problem of personal identity during the past fifteen years. I believe that my approach to this problem is quite different from the majority of analyses performed by Anglo-Americans in that it calls upon both the analytic and phenomenological traditions. Analytic expositions tend to be reductive in respect to that which serves as the criterion of the reidentification of the person. On the other hand, the phenomenological approach to the nature of the self seems to pay little heed to the problem of reidentification in its description of personhood and temporality. I try to weld together the best insights from both traditions on the question of personal identity.

In this study, I address the problem of personal identity by examining the possibility that a person is ascribed identity on the basis of having a supervenient self. Using the methods of non-eidetic phenomenology and analytic ontology, I argue that the self is supervenient on the physical and psychological properties of the human being. Understood in this manner, the self is not a static entity, but reflects the temporal nature of the person. Instead of trying to find the ground of personal identity in a purported static or relatively stable feature of the human being such as the soul, spatio-temporal continuity, or consciousness, I argue that the self is the 'pattern', 'character', or 'narrative identity' that is the outcome of a person's decision-making and actions.

It is the self as pattern or character that allows us to reidentify a human being as a specific person. In order to support this conclusion, I present arguments for viewing the self as a supervenient abstract particular or trope. Further the diachronic nature of the self demands a phenomenological description of time. However, a description of the temporal nature of a person is incomplete without an examination of how the social role of a human being contributes to the structure of the self. The social role needs to be interpreted in terms of morality and values as well.

For the sake of clarity and precision, I differentiate between consciousness and the self. A Sartrean interpretation of consciousness helps make this distinction.

I conclude the study with an argument against the improper use of thought experiments that shapes the discussion of personal identity in a way that tends to pay insufficient attention to the temporal, social, and moral nature of the self.

# 1 Introduction

The problem of personal identity has received considerable attention from philosophers for the past three decades. For the last two decades the discussion has been intensified because of Derek Parfit's arguments supporting his thesis that it is not personal identity in one's survival that matters but rather some degree of 'psychological continuity'. The latter can be understood as involving chains of overlapping memory experiences, intentional acts and results, and mental contents such as beliefs or desires that are not merely momentary.[1] Although I do not address directly the problem of personal identity as framed by Parfit, an underlying theme in this essay is that Parfit's understanding of the nature of personhood and of the self is attenuated. Although Parfit is concerned about the implications of the concept of personal identity for morality, he does not seem to see the importance of values, social roles, and the person's orientation to tensed time as essential elements involved in the reidentification of a person.

In contrast, it is my contention in this essay that it is the self understood as a 'pattern' or 'narrative identity' or dynamic 'Gestalt' that arises from the physical and psychological properties that serves as the basis for ascribing personal identity to ourselves and others. Further, I will argue that personal identity is a dynamic concept, i.e., a concept that involves an interpretation of the self as being a diachronic, supervenient 'abstract particular' or 'trope'. Moreover, the self, serving as the basis for the attribution of personal identity to human beings, cannot be understood apart from the influences coming to bear upon it from society in terms of values and customs. Those who treat the problem of personal identity as merely being a problem of how one and the same thing (a human being) can retain its identity over time in spite of internal and external changes taking place in respect to that being are destined to experience frustration if the frame of reference in which they operate is dictated by the model of non-conscious concrete particulars. Human beings that bear personhood are not mere 'lumps of meat'. Therefore, the problems attending the identity or reidentification of non-animate things, though having a bearing upon personal identity, are increased in number when one tries to understand what it is that allows us to reidentify a person.

In the following chapters, I will not produce a survey of the history of the problem of personal identity. This has been done many times in recent years. For example, Harold W. Noonan's *Personal Identity* is a very fine survey. Another helpful and recent survey is *Problems in Personal Identity* by James Baillie. A rather lengthy anthology edited by Daniel Kolak and Raymond Martin provides a representative sampling of recent literature on the subject. My intention in this essay is to attempt to account for the continued persistence of the belief in the concept of personal identity in spite of this concept having been called into question by David Hume and, in this century, by Derek Parfit and others. In Chapter II, I set the stage for the identification of that which serves as the basis for personal identity by indicating some of the challenges to this concept which, however, do not result in the dismissal of the everyday use of the concept. Instead of assuming that the person in the street is simply misguided in this matter, I search for a plausible reason why the notion of personal identity is retained.

As already indicated, I believe that the 'self' understood as a supervenient trope (abstract particular) is that which provides a basis for a person's reidentification over time. However, as a trope the self should not be understood as a static, timeless quality but as that which serves as the 'pattern' or 'narrative identity'[2] of the life of the person bearing that self. As such, the self can only be understood in terms of the temporality of the person. However, the groundwork for the latter point must be laid. Thus, Chapter III contains an exposition of the concept of supervenience as it must be understood in its role of depicting the relationship between the self and its subvenient properties, viz., the physical and psychological properties of the human individual that give rise to the self. However, the concept of supervenience itself needs a defense, and a *specific kind* of supervenience must be identified in order to serve in the role suggested.

To make my case, I must rely on recent literature that has discussed the body-mind problem in terms of the mind being a supervenient family of properties dependent upon the body (brain) and argue for the self being that which supervenes upon both the physical and the mental. The kind of supervenience that would support my version of the self, however, must be an asymmetrical and not a biconditional type of supervenience because the latter is extremely reductive in its implications. Thus, one must confront the work of Jaegwon Kim, who indeed asserts that supervenience must be understood as being biconditional. I perform an analysis of John Post's work on supervenience which supports the asymmetrical thesis, but Post's final position on the type of supervenience that is appropriate for the mind's dependency on the body is too weak for my understanding of the nature of the self.

In Part I of Chapter IV, I take a brief look at the work of George Stout and Donald Williams, two of the twentieth century's early proponents of abstract particulars. In doing so, however, my method is dialectical rather than merely expository. One of the major issues confronting the defender of abstract particulars is the necessity of the use of 'resemblance' in his/her interpretation of 'universals'. Thus, a worthy opponent of resemblance is Panayot Butchvarov, and I must counter his objections to a sufficient degree that the plausibility of the use of resemblance in respect to the classification of properties is defended against the concept of identity.

In Part II of Chapter IV, I defend the metaphysical nature of the self treated as a supervenient trope. Both Butchvarov and Keith Campbell provide useful contributions to this concept of the self, but both also raise serious questions about supervenience that demand a response before I can continue the analysis of the self. Butchvarov's 'cluster of qualities' notion and Campbell's 'tropes' provide support for my understanding of the self as a supervenient property. Yet, both philosophers are somewhat dubious about the necessity of appealing to the concept of supervenience in order to undertake an adequate analysis of abstract properties. I try to show that the dynamics of the self as a trope do not fit the traditional understanding of properties and that supervenience provides the proper conceptual vehicle for these dynamics. As will be seen, I cannot simply treat the self as an abstract property or universal per se inasmuch as any self has a uniqueness that would be lost if treated as a universal.

The contents of Chapter V serve as a necessary prelude to Chapters VI, VII, and VIII in the sense that the latter three chapters provide an analysis of the self as that which figures prominently in the person's being as it unfolds itself in time. Decision-making is one of the hallmarks of personhood, and thus in Chapter V I try to make a case, again relying upon portions of the body-mind literature, for the self's role in the causal process of intention and action – a process we understand as taking place within a physical context. Chapter V focuses on the problem of how the self can be an abstract particular and still have causal efficacy.

In Chapter VI, I try to show how the person is temporal through and through and how an existentialistic or phenomenological analysis of time must be taken into consideration in respect to the problem of personal identity. As the theme progresses in Chapter VI, it becomes clear that the

3

temporality of the self is not simply a private or individualistic matter. Rather, the self of the person does not arise solely from the individual but is also a product of the individual's interchange with society. Temporality and community are not separable components of personhood because the 'role' one plays out in his/her life (temporality) is in large measure a role provided by the community. G. H. Mead's work in respect to the social construction of the self is very helpful here if it is supplemented with a Sartrean understanding of consciousness.

Chapter VII continues the theme of the social self but with Ernst Tugendhat's interpretation of Mead's work serving as a transition (and as an improvement over Heidegger's understanding of the self's relationship to other selves) to Paul Ricoeur's ethical interpretation of the self. Ricoeur's work in turn is an improvement over that of Tugendhat's in that his emphasis upon values and community impacting upon the self is put in the context of the concept of 'narrative identity'. The latter is a way of talking about my notion of how the self helps constitute the person in a 'dynamic' way. Ricoeur performs an analysis of narrative identity within the context of the problem of personal identity and with Parfit's contribution to the discussion in mind. In fact, Ricoeur challenges Parfit at certain points but seems to capitulate to Parfit unnecessarily in the end. Be that as it may, Ricoeur's analysis of the self as 'narrative identity' incorporates both the temporality of the self stressed in Chapter VI and the social-ethical component stressed by Tugendhat. What emerges here, then, is the self as a supervenient trope but understood as the 'theme' or 'character' of the person's immersion in temporality.

In Chapter VIII, the relationship between the self and consciousness is explored. These two features of the person are not identical in function. Again, Mead and Sartre are very helpful in the examination of this relationship. Sartre's view of consciousness is an improvement upon Mead's even though the latter's position on the role of society in respect to the self is more helpful than Sartre's. I conclude the chapter with a brief look at Robert Nozick's analysis of the self's 'self-synthesis'. Much of what Nozick has to say in this regard is instructive and supportive of my view of the self as a supervenient trope, but unfortunately he backs off from endorsing this approach. I think that he would have been more supportive of this concept of self if he had kept separate the functions of self and consciousness, and if he had treated universals as abstract particulars.

Finally, in Chapter IX, I try to show that the philosophical demise of personal identity as generated by Parfit was misguided from the beginning because of his careless use of thought experiments. The thought experiments devised by Parfit have unfortunately shaped the direction of much of the recent discussion on the problem of personal identity. I do not claim that thought experiments should be banned in the analysis of concepts. For example, the discussions emerging from Putnam's 'Brain-in-a-Vat' and Searle's 'Chinese Room' experiments have been very fruitful. However, one must not let the thought experiment lose significant contact with the background conditions that serve as the context for the phenomenon under consideration. I contend that Parfit is guilty of this error. Of course, the point of using imaginative variation in respect to the properties of a phenomenon being investigated is to gain a better understanding of the nature of the phenomenon. But this cannot be accomplished if the background conditions are arbitrarily varied as well.

A word about the use of terminology is in order at this point. I have tried with great care not to use the terms 'person', 'human individual', 'human being', 'self', and 'consciousness' as synonyms. The term 'person' is not equivalent to the term 'self'. Neither is 'human being' nor 'human individual' nor 'individual' equivalent to 'person'. I use the term 'person' as signifying the human being or human individual that satisfies Dennett's six conditions of personhood with the added qualification that a person is necessarily 'temporal' as well. A human being (human individual or individual) is not necessarily a person. 'Human being', 'human individual', and 'individual' are terms used to refer merely to the organic, physical being of a person. The term 'self' refers to the 'character' or 'pattern' or 'narrative identity' that characterizes a particular person. But the term 'self' is not equivalent to the term 'consciousness' because the person bearing a specific self can be aware, to a certain extent, of the nature of its 'character' or 'narrative identity'. Furthermore, none of the preceding terms should be understood as being equivalent to 'transcendental ego'. The admonitions of Sartre against this are well taken; one must guard against an implicit idealism.

**Notes**

[1]   Derek Parfit, *Reasons and Persons* (Oxford: Clarendon Press, 1984), 204 ff.
[2]   A term taken from Paul Ricoeur. It suggests that the self is the product of one's interpretation of his/her life based on imaginative variant readings of personal decisions, cultural influences, and moral choices.

# 2 A brief look at the problem of personal identity

It is probably safe to say that the concept of personal identity is in a state of disarray. If the present philosophical endeavors in respect to an analysis of the nature of personal identity are any indication of the actual existence of something called personal identity, then Hume's perspective on the issue should not only be respected but honored as a negative method of investigation; i.e., since personal identity does not exist, there is no point in trying to discern its nature.

Nevertheless, there is something haunting about the notion of personal identity such that it seems to provoke constant renewals of investigations of the concept. Undoubtedly, during the era of Locke and Descartes, the concern about personal identity had its source in religious doctrine. That is to say, how can one be sure that eternal rewards or punishments are meted out to the right person(s)?[1] If a person changes both mentally and physically in a myriad of ways throughout a lifetime, then is the child the same as the subsequent middle-aged person, and is the middle-aged person the same as the subsequent elderly man or woman? Moreover, what does it mean for a person to persist in time when so many changes occur to that being? Thus, is it fair that the elderly person suffer eternal damnation for the 'mortal' sins committed by her youthful predecessor? Or, should the youthful predecessor receive the benefit of an eternal reward due to the supererogatory efforts of its elderly successor?

So Locke referred to the issue of personal identity as being of forensic concern.[2] Such a concern in his day and age was directed to a person's existence spanning more than an earthly time-line. However, we in our day

6

may still have a forensic concern about personal identity that is directed solely to our earthly span of existence even without a religious basis for that concern. (That is not to say that some persons today do not have the same concern for an afterlife evidenced during Locke's era.) Indeed, we can be concerned about mundane rewards or sanctions being meted out justly to a still living human being. For example, should Miss B be sentenced to life imprisonment for her part in a grisly murder that occurred three years ago? Miss B has changed considerably in the interim. She no longer is constituted by many of the cells that composed her body three years ago – not to mention the vast number of molecular changes that have occurred in her cells within the last hour. Further, during the three-year period from her commission of the crime to the day of sentencing, Miss B has undergone many and severe noticeable psychological changes. Some of these changes are: Her memory of the crime has dimmed, she has appropriated a belief in the respect for human life that was not part of her psychological make-up prior to the crime, and she now has feelings of guilt that were not in evidence until a year after the crime. It cannot be said of Miss B at this time that she is identical in all respects to the person who committed the heinous crime of three years ago. Thus, is it just for the present Miss B to be sentenced harshly on the basis of the acts performed by the former Miss B?

So, there can be judicial (and, more broadly, forensic) reasons for defending the existence of personal identity apart from religious reasons or concerns. Regardless of Hume's philosophical arguments against the existence of personal identity, we must contend with the persistence of the commonsensical tendency to identify the present Miss B with the Miss B of three years ago for no other reason than to be able to make an identification. Q: 'Is this the same person you knew as Miss B three years ago?' A: 'Yes'. Q: 'But, how can you make this claim? This person has changed molecularly, physiologically, and psychologically in a significant way in each case. She is undoubtedly a different person now from what she was three years ago?' A: 'I don't know about all that, but she is the same person'. Of course, no attorney for the defense would use such an argument (though Clarence Darrow attempted to defend Loeb and Leopold by espousing determinism). Our brief dialogue, of course, illustrates the fact that the person on the street refuses to give up the notion of personal identity in spite of obvious changes taking place between the person of yesterday and that of today.

Most of us would also refuse to give up the notion of our own personal identity even though we are willing to acknowledge the truth of a statement such as 'I am not the man/woman I used to be'. We are beings who have memories that seem to *belong* to us rather than simply being impersonal historical events. My memory, for some reason, means more to me than does a memory belonging to John Doe. (Witness my willingness to watch slides of my trip as opposed to my unwillingness to watch slides of John Doe's trip.) So we seem to give special attention or meaning to events that happen to us in contrast to those events that happen to other persons (family and friends excluded from this appraisal, of course). If there were not some kind of entity, property, or attribute that has special significance, that individuates us in a specific way from other entities, then why give special attention to those events or occasions that affect us immediately as opposed to those events that affect others?

My plans seem more important to me than the plans devised by John Doe for enactment by John Doe. Of course, if John Doe's plans impinge upon me, then I become quite interested in them. But why should this be the case? It would be too simple to say that the special attention given to my plans is an outcome or derivation of my instinct for survival.[3] In fact, one could just as well argue that one has an interest in survival for the sake of the implementation of one's plans. Further, it might be ventured that other animals have a special interest in their own survival without having a sense of personal identity. So there is no need to postulate personal identity as a reason for one's taking special interest in one's own plans. However, one can take special interest in plans that one devises for implementation after one's death. A will, a charitable foundation, a building, etc., can be the outcome(s) of a plan one has generated to come into effect after one's death. These plans have little bearing upon one's survival. To extend the notion of survival to that of the continued fame of one's name stretches the original rejoinder beyond credible recognition.

Even though one can point out many and severe problems with the notion of personal identity, there seem to be several reasons for the continued use of the notion. The problems with personal identity, however, are severe. Let us look at some of these problems as recognized by contemporary philosophers who use an analytic mode of investigation. (I am not classifying these philosophers as belonging to the analytical school of philosophy. I am simply using this term for want of a better one in respect to a certain kind of treatment of the problem of personal identity.)

I do not intend to give an exhaustive overview of the problem of personal identity. Harold W. Noonan has recently done that very thing in a very able way.[4] Nor do I want to establish the conceptual foundations of the treatment of personal identity. Sydney Shoemaker has done that in the contemporary classic *Self-Knowledge and Self-Identity*. What I want to do is to sketch the problems one has in maintaining the notion of personal identity if one accepts personal identity as a function of bodily identity.[5] I will also indicate problems with the position that identifies personal identity with 'psychological' continuity. Also, there are distinct problems (known for quite some time) that arise if one accepts personal identity as being due to a 'soul'

8

or self that is separate and distinct from the body.[6] This latter approach to personal identity is obviously dualistic in type, and body-mind dualism has generally been out of favor during the last several decades.

Having established the problems with the preceding three approaches to personal identity, I will present a case for personal identity as a kind of supervenience. This position will be materialistic (in a broad sense), but one hopes that it will not have the same problems other materialistic approaches have. In fact, it will explain why personal identity can be maintained in the face of physical gaps or interruptions in bodily continuity. At the same time, this position can also contend with problems faced by those who espouse personal identity on the basis of psychological continuity and by those who favor a dualistic approach.

Even though these positions take what appear to be diverse directions in their explanations of personal identity (whether it is physical [bodily] continuity, psychological continuity, or the 'simple' theory [continued soul, mind, substance, or self approach]), they all seem to assert the continued existence of *some thing* whether in terms of a unified substance (self or soul), or as the overlap of physical matter, or as continuing or overlapping psychological states or activities (such as memory). However, it is this assumption that generates many of the problems surrounding the notion of personal identity. With the use of thought-experiments and with the information coming from present-day psycho-neurological studies, the critic of the three main approaches to personal identity can generate many different problems in each case. If personal identity presupposes, as one would assume, a unity that individuates a human being from all other things, then incongruities develop in all three of the main expositions of personal identity.

In respect to the physical continuity position, one can raise questions about 'fission', an example being the splitting of the two hemispheres of the brain and reintroducing each hemisphere into two different cranial cavities (not medically possible at the present time but certainly empirically conceivable). Which body, then, bears the successor of the original intact brain? Or, if psychological continuity is at issue, then one can create a thought experiment such as the one developed by B.A.O. Williams, i.e., 'the reduplication argument' in which a person (let us call him B) in the twentieth century has memory-claims that fit those of Guy Fawkes of the sixteenth century.[7] It would appear that a reincarnation had taken place. But suppose not only had B appeared on the scene, but another individual, C, makes the very same claims and checks out as well as B does. Williams concludes that neither can be identified with Guy Fawkes (obviously due to the presupposition of unity being an essential factor in the definition of personal identity). However, Williams continues his criticism. If neither B nor C can be identified with

Guy Fawkes, then even if B existed by himself in the twentieth century, he should not be identified with Guy Fawkes. This is due to the belief that the identification of Guy Fawkes and B should depend upon their intrinsic relations and not on whether another external entity (C) exists. It would seem, then, that memory does not provide such 'intrinsic relations' and, therefore, cannot be the basis of personal identity in respect to a human being who has experienced physical changes in his/her body.

As far as the 'simple theory' (Noonan's term for the dualistic approach of soul and body) is concerned,[8] Locke already raised the problem of an immortal soul occupying different bodies. Would an advocate of the simple theory want to deny this as a logical possibility? And, if not, it would certainly seem to be clear that personal identity is not simply exhausted in the notion of a continuing (or immortal) soul or self. After all, a person's identity is not necessarily private to the person and to God. Thus if a soul were to occupy several bodies, then in what sense would the person's identity be cognizable by another observer?

Obviously, the preceding listing of difficulties attending the three major interpretations of personal identity is merely a tiny percentage of the total number of problems afflicting the three positions. My intention at this point has been simply to show that if each of these approaches is taken separately, then no one of the three can serve as a conclusive resolution or exposition of the notion of personal identity.

At this point, one is tempted simply to give up the concept of personal identity as did David Hume – at least in a philosophical sense. However, merely because a philosophical resolution to the problems of identifying the property(ies) by which personal identity is ascribed to a human being is not forthcoming quickly, there is no reason to deny the commonsensical use of the notion. For the reasons given above (and others), it is difficult to dismiss the notion, even though the three most popular approaches (physical, psychological, and simple) have severe problems in accounting for the ascription of personal identity to a human being. Thus, I want to suggest that a recent area of research in philosophy, viz., the concept of supervenience, may shed light on the problem of identifying the source of personal identity.[9]

As I see it, personal identity can best be understood not according to any simple feature or property of the human being, whether it is physical, psychological, or soul-like. Rather, the self is a supervenient abstract particular or trope that arises from and is dependent upon the melange of properties constituting a human being.[10] Yet, this supervenient trope is not identical with any one of these properties constituting any given human being. The supervenient trope in this case – the self – is dependent upon a collection of physical and psychological properties. My personal identity, for example, depends upon certain physical characteristics such as my peculiar

10

chromosomal make-up, my height, my skin color, etc., and also upon psychological features such as my memories, my beliefs (both occurrent and dispositional), my hopes, my dreams, my emotional dispositions, my plans, etc., culminating in a self that either persists in time or, more to the point, is constantly being constituted in time. Of course, a problem suggests itself immediately, i.e., if a trope (called the self) that is different from those properties just alluded to nevertheless arises from and is dependent upon them, then exactly which of these properties are essential (and which are not) to the identity of the self with the self in the transtemporal setting? Certainly, there must be a 'critical mass' of these properties that allows us to call Miss B of today the same Miss B of three years ago. In Chapter VII, we will see that the 'critical mass' is constituted by whatever properties provide an individual with a 'narrative identity'. At this point, let us take a very brief look at the history of the concept of supervenience.

The notion of supervenience in the contemporary period seems to date from the time of G. E. Moore and his defense of 'good' as a non-natural property.[11] Moore indicated that good 'followed from' the natural properties that could be discovered in a state of affairs that could be denominated as being good.

A later ethicist, R. M. Hare, seems to have been the first philosopher in the twentieth century to employ the term 'supervenience,' and, again, in a moral context. Since the time of these uses of the notion in a moral context, supervenience has proved to be useful in respect to a more perspicuous understanding of aesthetic properties in respect to a piece of art,[12] and in respect to the body-mind problem, i.e., the idea of the mind being supervenient upon the body.[13]

In a cursory way, I would like to show why the appeal to supervenience seems to fare better than the three main approaches to personal identity. As far as the physical approach is concerned, undoubtedly, no one would want to deny that the physical contributes in a significant way to the constitution of a specific personal identity. In the first place, if the body of a person we know changes in a radical way over a specific period of time, we may be shocked and find it difficult to believe that P(2) is the same person as the P(1) we used to know. Cancer, AIDS, disfiguring accidents, the aging process, etc., can all contribute to our disbelief in such a case. Yet we would not refuse to identify P(1) with P(2) if P(1) were to suffer the loss of a leg, both legs, an arm, or both legs and both arms. We would continue to claim that P(2) is P(1) in spite of a radical physical transformation. Of course, a response could be that regardless of radical changes in the body of a given human being we would continue to identify that person as the same because the most important physical part of the human is the brain. So long as the brain is intact, the person persists through time (even in spite of molecular and cellular

11

transformations). After all, the brain is the physical locus of the person's mental states, including hopes, passions, emotions, thoughts, character and personality traits, beliefs, plans and projections into the future, etc. However, difficulties arise when extrapolations from split-brain experimentation occur. If the two hemispheres of the brain are separated and each is placed in a different cranial cavity, do we have two individuals, P(2) and P(3), both claiming identity with P(1)? But this would violate the presupposition of unity that we acknowledge as a condition of personal identity. So physical continuity cannot be the sole condition of personal identity.

However, one should notice that the preceding focus on the brain as the bearer of personal identity really involves psychological continuity as well. The thought experiment of two individual beings, not only having physical continuity with P(1) on the basis of each having one of the hemispheres of P(1), also becomes problematic in the sense that these two individual beings have the very same hopes, plans, personality and character traits, etc., upon which psychological continuity depends. Thus, the split brain extrapolation not only calls into question the belief that the physical is the bearer of personal identity but the belief that psychological continuity is *the* bearer of personal identity.

Nevertheless, we would not want to say that psychological factors do not help contribute to the notion of personal identity. Suppose we knew a person by the name C(1) and our knowledge of this person spanned two decades with very frequent contact, with many social experiences and many deep 'heart to heart' talks. Would we not have a very difficult time believing that C(2) was C(1) if (after a short period of time passed, say a month, during which we had no contact with C(1)) C(2) manifested strong differences in attitudes toward other persons (not only verbal but behavioral), reflected extremely different goals and plans for his/her future, and demonstrated quite different emotional responses in situations similar to those we had experienced with C(1)? Undoubtedly, we would be tempted to take another look at the physical characteristics of this person in order to make sure that an impostor had not attempted to fool us into believing that it is C(1). Even if C(2) looked like C(1) and we had demonstrated to us that the finger prints and DNA of C(1)and C(2) were identical, would we not be tempted to say that C(1) and C(2) are not the same person?

It would appear that the continuity of both the physical and psychological properties of an individual are necessary to his/her personal identity, but neither kind of continuity by itself is sufficient for the ascription of personal identity to an individual. And, of course, neither is the simple theory (the soul or substance approach) sufficient, as has already been demonstrated with the logical possibility of a soul inhabiting more than one body. We would be confused as to the personal identity of an individual if the body were not taken into consideration and the sole consideration would be an immaterial substance of some sort. The immaterial substance, in order to individuate the person who is the outcome of the soul inhabiting a certain body, would have to manifest those very characteristics we associate with the psychological continuity approach. Undoubtedly, personal identity is a matter of individuation. To ascribe personal identity to a human being without that person having individuating characteristics seems incomprehensible. A 'soul' as a bare datum simply does not provide the kind of characteristics by which a person's identity is individuated. Of course, if one subscribes to the notion that the 'soul' is that upon which characteristics may be 'hung' and, thereby, affords the necessary individuating characteristics, one would have to ask the 'Humean' question as to why those characteristics ascribed to the bare soul are not sufficient in their own right in performing the function of individuation? Further, it would seem that the only thing that would allow a differentiation between bare souls (apart from the psychological characteristics that according to this theory are not integral to the soul) would be their respective spatial locations. But souls are supposedly not constrained by spatial conditions. Thus, it is conceivable that two or more souls could inhabit the same space (same body).

Now, even though there is clearly a distinction between the bearer of personal identity and how one knows the bearer of personal identity, in this case the proponent of the simple theory would have to show how an observer could distinguish between Soul(1) and Soul(2) which are both inhabiting the same body. Once again, at best, one would have to refer to the psychological properties (already mentioned) that adhere to both souls in question in order for a differentiation to take place in respect to the persons occupying one and the same body.

But from the observer's point of view, the practical outcome would be an example of a schizoid personality. In such a case, the personal identity of the human in question would be treated as a person with multiple personalities. (Actually, the psychological term would be 'multiple identities'.) Such a situation, however, is treated as an abnormality, and one would hope that the human in question would be able to achieve an integration and/or eradication of some of the warring characteristics. The ideal is still one consistent, unified personality. The point I am trying to make is that personal identity in an ideal sense involves an integrated, consistent kind of grouping of characteristics. And the bare-soul approach, since it does not espouse the notion that the continuity of psychological characteristics constitutes personal identity, must account for how the observer can be in a position to cognize the individuating characteristics of the bare soul.

However, if the proponent of the simple theory does not postulate a bare-soul thesis but instead postulates a soul that includes psychological characteristics, then the critic has the right to ask the question: If we individuate according to the psychological characteristics that supposedly belong to a soul, then what practical function does the soul itself perform in respect to the constitution of personal identity? The soul seems to be superfluous in this case.

Thus, this argument revolving around the simple theory brings us to the point of saying that even though neither the physical nor the psychological characteristics in terms of continuity are sufficient taken by themselves in the constitution of personal identity, both are necessary (but not in the sense of any single specific physical or psychological property) to personal identity. And, therefore, in our consideration of the role these characteristics play in respect to the supervenient nature of the self, we can safely ignore the simple theory.

Now, the reason the concept of supervenience is so salutary in respect to the problem of personal identity is that, whereas both the physical and psychological theories of personal identity suffer shipwreck as soon as an example of a physical or psychological discontinuity is presented (thereby reflecting a disunity that personal identity cannot allow if it is to be personal *identity*), the self as a trope that supervenes upon the physical and psychological properties belonging to an individual can allow for some 'gaps' and 'losses in the base or subvening properties. That is to say, even though physical and psychological properties as a 'family of properties' are necessary for the generation of the self, the loss of any one or even several properties would not eliminate the particular self that supervenes upon the subvening properties. For example, the loss of a leg does not cause a loss of personal identity, the loss of memories of events that took place in 1962 does not constitute (at least in my case) a loss of personal identity, a change in long-term plans for one's future is not a loss of personal identity, etc. Of course, there must be a limit to the gaps, losses, and changes in the subvening properties from which the self arises beyond which personal identity will be in jeopardy or lost.

Exactly where such a boundary can be located is, in the case of personal identity, not as easily determined as it might be in a moral context. For example, in a moral context we might say that a morally upright person manifests the following virtues: wisdom, temperance, prudence, courage, honesty, sincerity, veracity, chastity, tolerance, and forgiveness. (I doubt that the preceding list is exhaustive.) So, moral rectitude supervenes upon the preceding qualities. A person might not exemplify wisdom, prudence, courage, and even chastity (in some cases) and still be considered morally upright. Yet, if honesty, veracity, and temperance were not manifest, then I suspect moral rectitude would no longer be in evidence. To attempt the same identification of the limit in respect to the self, however, strikes me as an almost impossible task to achieve. Yet in principle such a determination must be possible; otherwise the notion of supervenience relative to personal identity must be considered vacuous.

It is too facile to make claims for supervenience in dealing with the crucial problem facing the other theories of personal identity and not allow for cases where the supervenient self *does not* arise from a grouping of *possible* subvenient properties. After all, the notion of supervenience itself is a concept in which the generated property is in fact dependent upon (even though distinguishable from) the subvenient properties. That is, if you do not have the subvenient properties (and, probably, in proper relationships with one another), you will not have the supervenient property. So not everything is permissible in this case.

Of course, the only way to determine whether the supervenient self is lost whenever certain subvenient properties are missing would be by a case-by-case inspection. However, I can state in broad terms when changes in subvenient properties would result in a loss of personal identity, and the preceding difficulties mentioned in respect to the positions of physical continuity and psychological continuity are anticipatory. In the first place, I think it is plausible to assert that personal identity is lost whenever there is a 'significant gap' in the causal-spatial continuity of the physical characteristics of the individual in question. A serious gap in physical continuity is illustrated by Williams' Guy Fawkes example. B(1) would not be identified with Fawkes in spite of the correspondence of B(1)'s memory with the events that happened to Fawkes. It would make no difference to us whether B(1)'s 'memory' conformed to historical accounts of Fawkes' life. We would still declare Fawkes and B(1) to be different *persons*, and we would attempt to explain B(1)'s alleged accurate memory on bases other than that of personal identity. B(1) may have read an historical account of Fawkes' life and forgot that he had read it. B(1) may have absorbed the telling of Fawkes' adventures by a schoolmaster and forgot that he had heard it, etc.

If B(1)'s memory goes beyond the extant historical renderings of Fawkes' life and times, thereby suggesting first-hand experiences, we will promptly discount these alleged memories inasmuch as we have no way to verify them.

In the second place, psychological continuity is also a necessary element belonging to the subvenient properties. As was mentioned above, if an individual P(1) manifests a sweeping change in personality characteristics, emotional characteristics, etc., we would tend to check the physical characteristics of the individual in question more closely in order to make sure that an impostor is not attempting to confuse us. This is really a more difficult situation than is the case of a gap in physical continuity. First, it should be obvious that the psychological properties are dependent upon the physical, i.e., the brain. Second, the very fact that we would tend to check the

15

physical properties of the individual whose identity is in question (due to psychological changes) suggests that we see the physical as primary. Nevertheless, if an individual (say, for example, 'Sam') were to manifest striking changes in his attitudinal, emotional, and other psychological characteristics while we were convinced that his body retained physical continuity with the body that bore the old psychological characteristics, most of us would be perplexed by the change in Sam's 'personhood'. After a period of adjustment, we would respond to and act toward Sam on the basis of his newly appropriated psychological characteristics. If an old acquaintance of Sam's who had not seen him in quite some time should happen to mention to us that Sam is acting strangely, we who experienced Sam's transition to his present state would most likely say something to the effect: 'Oh, yes. Sam is a changed person. He is no longer the avaricious, self-centered, etc., person we once knew.' Even though Sam is the same individual in terms of physical continuity, he is not the *same* person.

The preceding bit of dialogue is not intended to illustrate the 'contextual analysis of 'person,' but how the term 'person' is used surely sheds light upon what constitutes the nature of personal identity. If either physical discontinuity or psychological discontinuity serves to alter our impressions of the personhood of a given individual, then it behooves us to start thinking in terms of collections of properties comprising the basis for a supervenient self rather than in terms of some single linear continuity being the sole characteristic of personal identity. Even more important, personal identity is best understood in supervenient terms inasmuch as some changes, gaps, and losses may occur in respect to subvenient properties without our declaring that a new person has come into existence.

In the next chapter, I will argue for the kind of supervenience demanded by the concept of self treated as a supervenient trope; it should be non-reductive and asymmetrical. These characteristics are usually associated with what the literature calls 'strong' supervenience as opposed to other forms known as 'weak' and 'global' supervenience.

### Notes

[1] See John Locke, *An Essay Concerning Human Understanding* (Oxford: Clarendon Press, 1975), ed. Peter Nidditch, Book II, C. 27, Secs. 13-15.

[2] See Locke, op. Cit. II, 27, Sec. 26.

[3] See Parfit's argument against the belief that we should give special attention to our own interests based on a notion of literal personal identity in *Reasons and Persons*, pp. 345-347.

[4] Harold W. Noonan, *Personal Identity* (London: Routledge, 1989).

[5] Noonan, 2-8, points out that there are three possible ways of

interpreting bodily continuity: 1) the body, 2) the brain (in its entirety), and 3) the physical (meaning by this term portions of the brain).

[6] See Locke's *Essay*, II, 27, Secs. 6 and 14, in which he indicates some of the problems with personal identity being based on the soul or substance approach.

[7] B.A.O. Williams, *Problems of the Self* (Cambridge: Cambridge University Press, 1973), 7-12.

[8] Noonan, 18ff.

[9] Jaegwon Kim is well-known for his many articles on supervenience. A summarizing article on the topic is 'Concepts of Supervenience', *Philosophy and Phenomenological Research* 45, 2 (December 1984): 257-270.

[10] The theory of abstract particulars or tropes denies that the properties belonging to a particular object are universals. Rather, the properties of the particular object are particulars in their own right. That is to say, a physical object, for example, is a 'cluster' of such abstract particulars or tropes. See Keith Campbell's *Abstract Particulars* (Oxford: Basil Blackwell, 1990, 3-4.

[11] Kim, 258-261.

[12] Ibid., 259-260.

[13] Ibid., 260.

# 3 Searching for the proper kind of supervenience

If one believes that there are too many problems with a dualistic interpretation of the body-mind relationship and at the same time believes that the person is not merely identical with the physical body and its activities, then it becomes very difficult indeed to find a philosophical concept that sheds light upon a dependency relationship that allows both relata (body and self) to remain distinct even though one is dependent upon the other. For this reason, it seems natural to turn to the concept of supervenience to provide the necessary structural arrangement described in the preceding sentence, i.e., an asymmetrical dependency relationship with the distinctness of the relata remaining intact. What is desired is some concept that can do justice to the notion of the self as being dependent upon physical and psychological properties of the human being without the self being considered just another one of the physical and/or psychological properties of the human being. A question may be raised at this point. What would be wrong with considering the 'self' as being one or more of the psychological properties of the human being? Why not consider memory and/or consciousness and/or self-consciousness, etc., as the self, thereby eliminating the need for the search for some philosophical concept that links dependency and distinction? The answer lies in the fact that the fully functioning person, the human being that can be said to have a self, does not only have the psychological characteristics mentioned above but also has the dynamic power of integrating all of its physical and psychological properties by making decisions for its future. Facing the future and making decisions in respect to the future (another term for this human capacity is 'self-constitution') is not simply another one of the psychological properties (such as consciousness) per se because this capacity must in turn take the psychological properties into consideration in performing its decision-making duties. In other words, even if decision-making is a psychological property, it is of a higher order that in itself demands our recognition. It is still necessary, therefore, to come to grips with an asymmetrical dependency relationship that does justice to retaining a distinction between relata.

So, does the concept of supervenience provide us with the appropriate philosophical concept by which we may interpret the relationship existing between the self and the properties belonging to the human being? The initial use to which the concept was put in the twentieth century, i.e., the relationship between descriptive or natural properties and ethical properties, seemed promising at first glance for our purposes as well. G. E. Moore is quoted by Jaegwon Kim:

> ...if a given thing possesses any kind of intrinsic value in  a certain degree, then not only must that same thing possess it, under all circumstances, in the same degree, but also anything exactly like it, must, under all possess it in exactly the same degree.[1]

Kim also refers to Hare (whom Kim believes to be the twentieth-century philosopher that gave currency to the term 'supervenience') for further use of the concept in respect to values:

> First, let us take that characteristic of 'good' which has been called its supervenience. Suppose that we say 'St. Francis was a good man'. It is logically impossible to say this and to maintain at the same time that there might have been another man placed exactly in the same circumstances as St. Francis, and who behaved in exactly the same way, but who differed from St. Francis in this respect only, that he was not a good man.[2]

In this case, then, the property 'good' supervenes upon the base (subvenient) properties such as certain kinds of acts by St. Francis in certain kinds of circumstances. If the kinds of acts differ – e.g., St. Francis begins to twist the necks of birds for no apparent reason rather than feeding the birds – then it is extremely unlikely that the term 'good' will remain applicable to the situation depicted. In other words, the relation of supervenience involves the notion of 'covariance'. Kim says:

> Supervenient properties covary with their subvenient, or base, properties. In particular, indiscernibility in respect of the base

properties entails indiscernibility in respect of the supervenient properties.[3]

Covariance, then, would seem to be a necessary feature of supervenience. If a family of properties (A) supervenes upon a family of properties (B), then in the case of a family of properties (C) exactly similar to that of (B), one may expect to find another family of properties exactly similar to that of (A). It seems clear in the quotations from Moore and Hare above that covariance is a characteristic of supervenience.

Covariance as a characteristic of supervenience is even more clearly evident in D. M. Armstrong's definition of supervenience in A Combinatorial Theory of Possibility:

> If there exist possible worlds which contain an entity or entities R, and if in each such world there exists an entity or entities S, then and only then S supervenes on R. For instance, if there exist worlds in which two or more individuals have the property F, then, in each world containing such states of affairs, these same individuals stand in the relation of resemblance (at least in some degree). These resemblances are therefore supervenient on the individuals in question having property F.[4]

This definition is characterized by Armstrong as being simple', and I would agree that it is too simple to deliver the full flavor of the nature of supervenience. However, it does illustrate the point that supervenience has covariance as a characteristic. Armstrong says, "This definition allows there to be cases where not only is S supervenient upon R, but R is at the same time supervenient upon S".[5] As Armstrong points out, this reciprocal supervenience does not hold for the example of supervenience he gave following the definition. However, this particular definition does reflect covariance in an obvious way.

If covariance were the only characteristic of supervenience, however, it would not serve very well for the purposes of those who discern in cases of the psychical supervening upon the physical a dependency relationship as well. Kim attributes to Donald Davidson's article 'Mental Events' the introduction of two more characteristics of supervenience, viz., dependency and nonreducibility.[6] Dependency is a relation that is important to those working in either the area of the philosophy of mind or the area of personhood or self-constitution who do not accept dualistic theories in respect to the body-mind problem or the self-body relationship and at the same time do not want to be considered eliminativists. It seems to me that covariance could be a relation perfectly at home within a dualistic frame of reference. For example, in respect to the simple theory (a theory that proposes that a soul can exist that is independent of the body), it is conceivable that as the properties informing the soul vary, so do those properties informing the body, and vice versa. But for those of us who find too many problems with the notion of an autonomous soul relative to the body, the relation of dependency in respect to the self supervening upon the body is indispensable. An asymmetry in respect to the families of properties is necessary. Family (A) not only covaries with family (B), but if family (B) does not exist, then family (A) does not exist, i.e., covariance is not a guarantee of the dependency relation as Kim points out.[7] Covariance does not necessarily mean that there are "property-to-property correlations between supervenient and subvenient properties".[8] In the case of mental phenomena (family (A)) supervening upon neural conditions within the brain (family (B)), if family (B) did not exist, then neither would family (A), but not necessarily the converse. For example, the supervenient property 'itch' could exist due to an inflamed area on the leg; it could also exist even though the leg does not (the phantom limb syndrome). Likewise, with the self (family (A)), if certain psychical and physical properties (family (B)) did not exist, then neither would the self. Suppose there were a case of severe brain damage so that the human being in question did not have the capacity of self-consciousness; then that being would not have a self.

What is problematic at this point is the matter of getting clear about the range of variation allowed in family (B) without losing family (A). If one looks at the supervenient property of 'good', for example, it is obvious that one could have many different groupings of properties serving as subvenient properties for the appropriate ascription of the term 'good'. One could observe a boy scout assisting an elderly person across the street and deem the consequences good. One could observe a customer returning money to a waitress after she had shortchanged herself and deem the consequences good. In each case, good supervenes upon certain conditions that are quite different one from the other. So certain supervenient properties are not unique in depending upon properties of family (B), yet in specific cases, if family (B) did not exist, then family (A) would not have been exemplified in those cases. This fact is encouraging because it allows the possibility that in respect to the self supervening upon certain psychical and physical properties, the latter may change without the former becoming a different self. That is to say, different groupings of properties of family (B) may still give rise to the same supervenient property(ies).

It would seem, then, that the kind of supervenience desired by those working in the area of self-constitution or by non-dualistic physicalists working with the body-mind problem is a supervenience that allows an asymmetrical dependency relation as well as covariance. Kim raises the very important question of whether the covariance of supervenient and subvenient properties is compatible with the notion of dependency. It should be obvious from the preceding paragraph that different groupings of base properties can give rise to the same supervenient property(ies). Not only do different groupings of base properties provide the same supervenient property in respect to certain valuational situations, but different groupings of base properties can give rise to the same kind of mental phenomenon. Functionalism (a theory pertaining to the philosophy of mind) has shown that different physical properties and/or conditions can support the same kind of function. Computers with the appropriate software can add a series of numbers as can the human brain provide a sum for the same numbers. These examples of a dependency relation indicate that the same supervenient property may occur given different groupings of subvenient properties. How can this kind of dependency relation be considered compatible with covariance? Kim speaks to this very question.[9] He indicates that strong covariance (a covariance holding across possible worlds and not restricted to the world under consideration) is not in itself an asymmetric relation (nor a symmetric one either). Thus, strong covariance in both directions (supervenient varying with the subvenient and the subvenient varying with the supervenient) will not provide the needed asymmetrical dependence relation. Kim also presents arguments against a strong covariance in one direction as providing the desired dependency relation. Of course, it is strong covariance in one direction that seems to fit the above examples of dependency relations. Formally, Kim describes one-way strong covariance:

> A-properties depend on B-properties just in case A strongly covaries with B, but not conversely; that is, any B-indiscernible things are A-indiscernible but there are A-indiscernible things that are B-discernible.[10]

Kim asks this question of the above proposal: 'Can we count on A to depend on B whenever A strongly covaries with B and B does not depend on A?'[11] He answers the question in the negative:

> What this argument neglects, rather glaringly, is the possibility that an explanation of the covariance from A to B may be formulated in terms of a third set of properties. It seems clearly possible for there to be three sets of properties A, B, and C, such that A and B each depend on C, A covaries with B but B does not covary with A, and A does not depend on B. Something like this could happen if although both A and B covary with C, B makes finer discriminations than A, so that indiscernibility in regard to B-properties entails indiscernibility with respect to A, but not conversely.[12]

22

Does this mean, then, that the relation of supervenience cannot include within its repertoire of elements an asymmetrical dependency relation? After all, Kim himself believes that covariance is the most important feature of supervenience.[13]   No, not at all.   As Kim points out, the concept of supervenience may contain both elements. The relation of dependence has ontological significance whereas covariance is metaphysically neutral. Kim's claim, then, is that supervenient dependence is not derivable from covariance.

Thomas R. Grimes in his article 'Supervenience, Determination, and Dependency' attempts to make a distinction between determination and dependency – a distinction, he claims, that is not acknowledged by Kim.   In the course of defending this distinction, Grimes indicates that it is possible for both kinds of supervenience, i.e., determination and dependency supervenience, to have different groupings of base properties, each of which gives rise to the same supervenient property:

> Part of the attraction of determination supervenience is that it allows for multiple subvening bases;  that is, the same supervening property can be associated with a variety of subvening properties from the same family of properties.  This aspect is especially appealing when dealing with the relation between the mental and physical insofar as it seems that the same mental state could be induced by different physical states. Dependency supervenience also affords this type of flexibility.  That is, since dependency supervenience requires objects (worlds) that are I-indiscernible with respect to A to be only partially I-indiscernible with respect to B, the subvening bases can vary without limit provided they share at least one B type property.   In the case of the mental's supervening on the physical, the physical property common to each subvening base could be something like the property of having mass.[14]

Besides covariance and dependency, Kim asserts that many philosophers also believe that supervenience includes another feature, viz., nonreducibility.

The question of nonreducibility traditionally turns on whether a given scientific theory can be explained in terms of another theory (the reducing theory).   Kim points out that there is some question about whether the concept of supervenience does involve nonreducibility.[15] He believes that the notion of nonreducibility in respect to supervenience was given currency by Moore and Hare:

> [W]ell known for their supervenience thesis concerning the moral relative to the naturalistic, [Moore and Hare] also formulated classic

and influential arguments against ethical naturalism, the doctrine that the moral is definitionally reducible to the naturalistic.[16]

Kim believes that the question of nonreducibility in respect to supervenience is not so much concerned with 'definitional' reducibility as it is with 'nomological' reducibility, and he receives this impression from Donald Davidson's anomalous monism as represented in his article 'Mental Events'. Of course, in this article Davidson rejects the notion that it is possible to identify laws that correlate mental phenomena with physical phenomena (brain states).

Kim, however, believes that a supervenience that includes strong covariance in its repertoire of features is, in fact, an example of a supervenience that does allow the supervenient property to be considered reducible to the subvening properties. Kim refers to the notion of 'the condition of strong connectibility' to establish his point. This condition is stated as follows:

> Each primitive predicate P of the theory being reduced is connected with a coextensive predicate Q of the reducer in a biconditional law of the form: 'For all x, Px iff Qx'; and similarly for all relational properties.[17]

If this condition applies to the 'bridge laws' (those statements connecting key terms between the reducing and reducible theories), then reducibility is possible. Kim claims that strong connectibility is found in cases of strong covariance.

In the case of strong covariance, the appropriate subvenient properties and supervenient properties mutually entail one another. This mutual entailment is based, however, on Kim's belief that disjunction is an allowable way of forming properties. He acknowledges that some philosophers disagree with him on this issue, i.e., that disjunction does not preserve 'this crucial feature of propertyhood'[18], viz., resemblance among the properties in question. Kim responds:

> I do not find these arguments compelling. It isn't at all obvious that we must be bound by such a narrow and restrictive conception of what nomic properties, or properties in general, must be in the present context. When reduction is at issue, we are talking about theories, theories couched in their distinctive theoretical vocabularies. And it seems that we allow, and ought to allow, freedom to combine and recombine, the basic theoretical predicates and functors by the usual logical and mathematical operations available in the underlying language, without checking each step with something like the

24

resemblance criterion; that would work havoc with free and creative scientific theorizing.[19]

For our purposes, I do not believe that anything crucial turns on whether the self in its capacity for self-constitution is 'reducible' to its base or subvenient properties.

Suppose it were the case that biology is reducible to physics and chemistry. Does this reducibility eliminate the distinctive demands or needs of certain macro operations in biology? No, of course not. Identifying a 'gene' with a 'chromosome' does not eliminate the computations connected with making a prediction about the outcomes of cross-fertilization of different varieties of seed corn. Reducibility does not mean elimination. Reducibility still allows for the making of distinctions between the reducing and reducible theories. And, certainly, the self is distinguishable from (although possibly reducible to) the memory, the body per se, consciousness, etc.

John Post in his recent works, The Faces of Existence (1987) and Metaphysics: A Contemporary Introduction (1991), provides us with a model for the self as a supervenient property with his treatment of 'nonreductive unifications'.[20] I think it is safe to say that Post is referring to mental events as the primary nonreducible phenomena when he indicates that it is conceivable that one could have a physicalistic interpretation of the body's primacy in respect to thoughts or intentionality or feelings without these phenomena being 'nothing but' physical phenomena:[21]

> [A] person or thing can have many kinds of properties that are irreducibly different, properties that are not in any relevant sense equivalent. Not only can things have the physical and other properties studied by the natural sciences or their equivalents. Things can also have properties not equivalent to any physical properties, including certain mental, intentional, cultural, and historical properties, to mention only a few. Some physicalists even argue that there are moral and other normative properties that things objectively have. Nonreductive physicalism is therefore congenial with a thoroughgoing pluralism as regards kinds of properties, even though it affirms a monism of underlying entities and processes.[22]

So Post is arguing for the notion that mental events et al can be traced back to physical conditions without the mental being reduced to the physical.

But Post wants to stay within the physicalist camp even though a serious question arises, viz., How can we retain the irreducibility of the mental without falling into a dualism of the mind and body? Post will have to be able to defend the concept that the physical can 'determine' the mental without

25

the mental being reducible to the physical. He wants to defend a nonreductive 'determination'. Post uses the term 'determination' more often than 'supervenience' primarily because it connotes in popular usage a sense of one thing's dependence upon another. In contrast, some dictionaries treat 'supervenience' as meaning 'extraneous upon', and this interpretation does not reflect the desired relation of dependence:[23]

> The basic idea is simple enough. In everyday language, when we say that one state of affairs determines another, we mean that how the first is settles or fixes how the second can be. Given the way the first is, there is one and only one way the second can be.[24]

Post is aware that Kim, among others, does not believe that the physical can determine the nonphysical without the nonphysical being reducible to the physical. Post formalizes the supervenience relation in the following way, calling it D1:

> D1 – Given any two physically possible worlds W1 and W2, and given any two things x and y, if x has the same physical properties in W1 as y has in W2, then x has the same nonphysical properties in W1 as y has in W2.[25]

Post indicates that it is not necessary to assume that D1 entails that a connective generalization be in effect between the physical properties and the nonphysical properties. That is to say, one need not believe that whatever has P (physical property) also has N (nonphysical property) on the basis of D1. Post indicates that the reductionist uses the notion of connective generalization to defend the reducibility of N to P. The following abstract counterexample, in Post's estimation, indicates the possibility of physical properties determining nonphysical properties without a connective generalization being in effect, thereby allowing for the nonreducibility of nonphysical properties:

> Now let's take on the abstract counterexample against the claim that determination in the sense of D1 entails that for each realized N there is some physical P such that whatever has P has N. . . . Let there be two worlds W1 and W2, two objects x and y, one P-property P', and one N-property N'. . . . Suppose further that in W1, x and y both have P', and x but not y has N'; and that in W2, x but not y has P' and neither has N'. . . . This example is consistent with D1 but inconsistent with the connective generalization. . . . Since the only physical property here is P', there is no P such that whatever has P has N'. For even though x

and y have the same P-properties in W1, y has P' but not N' in W1 and so too for x in W2.[26]

Post anticipates the objection that if the connective generalization is not necessarily operable in all cases of physical properties determining nonphysical properties, then 'what evidence could we ever have to support the claim of determination or dependency?'[27] Nonreductive dependency would simply turn out to be a brute fact. Sometimes that which has P also has N; sometimes not. Post responds on behalf of the nonreductive physicalist with the question: Why is not connective generalization (whatever has P has N) just as much a brute fact as nonreductive dependency? Why is not connective generalization just as much in need of an explanation as is nonreductive dependency?[28]

Post argues further that determination can be discerned between P and N properties without a connective generalization being involved. One way of discerning such determination is through observation: 'We may observe repeatedly that two cells that are the same in relevant physical respects are the same in some given biological respect'.[29] Another example: 'Or two organisms alike in relevant neurological respects may be observed always to be alike as regards their learning ability'.[30] He wants to claim that the correlation in the two examples need not imply a connective generalization just as the 'abstract counterexample' above does not imply a connective generalization even though one can discern a determination correlation in the properties exemplified by x and y.

Post also claims that besides observation providing evidence for the determination of a state of affairs by another without calling upon connective generalization, one can also point to the existence of connective theories. Such theories 'usually grow out of attempts to unify and systematize the otherwise miscellaneous observed correlations between the two kinds of phenomena'.[31] Post claims that such theories:

often entail not only that a given kind or class of N-phenomena is determined by some underlying P-phenomena. They often entail as well that there is no P-property P such that whatever has P has a given N-property N . . . . Thus connective theories often contain no connective generalizations. In this way we can have evidence that the P-properties determine the N-properties, even though we have no evidence for (and indeed some against) the connective generalization that whatever has P has N. Or so the nonreductive determinationist will try to argue.[32]

I really do not understand why Post is struggling so hard to defend the possibility of what he calls N-properties not necessarily occurring whenever the relevant P-properties occur. Perhaps he insists upon this point because he identifies reductivism with 'nothing-butism'. But even if he makes this identification, he need not argue as indicated above. Taking a page from his biological examples, we can argue that one who is not blinded by 'eliminativistic' presuppositions can surely see that the biological properties involved in two animals copulating are not the same as the physical properties that are descriptive of the couple even though the former are dependent upon the latter. The latter involves such factors as two masses of such and such a weight with such and such a momentum making contact in a particular spatio-temporal slice, etc., whereas the biological properties involve such items as spermatozoa, ova, ovulation, conception, etc. If the confirmed reductivist insists that I simply have not taken all of the physical properties constituting the biological level into consideration, then I can reply (in some instances) that the couple under consideration is a human couple who have purposively engaged in this act at this time not out of instinct and not for pleasure, but because they have been childless for the first ten years of their marriage and this is an act of desperation. Try using a purely physical description in this case and see if you can capture all of the relevant properties!

If the preceding attempt is not convincing, we can indicate that reductivism need not be interpreted only in ontological terms, but in nomological terms as well. It may be the case that the biological properties mentioned above (but not the 'personal' reasons) may be understood ultimately in terms of physical laws, but that does not mean that biological properties do not exist in a distinctive way. Events we deem to be biological in type may correlate so well with the laws of physics and chemistry that whenever the latter are applicable to certain micro-level conditions, we will be able to predict a specific biological event or process. Yet the possibility of such a prediction from one level to the next does not eliminate the properties of the emergent level.

Post also argues in a strange manner using Ruth Millikan's biosemantical approach. That is, he wants to claim that

> [t]here are plenty of cases in which a nonphysical property of a thing – a biological property, for example – is not determined by the thing's own physical properties, so that two things that are physically indiscernible can have different biological properties. Recall from Chapter 3 the biological notion of the proper function or purpose of an organ or device or behavior. What the proper function of an organ is, we saw, is a matter of a history. To have a given proper function the

organ must be a reproduction of an ancestor in a family of organs, which family historically proliferated because a critical mass of the ancestors performed that function.[33]

Post is claiming that an organ's proper function is not solely determined by its physical properties and its causal powers. Rather, the history of this organ contributes to its function. Suppose one had serious heart problems so that a transplant operation is considered a necessary precaution. According to Post's position, even if there were some 'cosmic accident' by which an exact duplicate of one's heart were to materialize so that the operation could take place, the item in question would still not be a heart. I find this extremely puzzling. I do not deny that the history surrounding an entity – in particular a self – contributes to the relational nature of the entity. In fact, Post argues this very point (again relying on Millikan). That is, suppose a cosmic accident were to materialize an exact duplicate of one's physical being next to you. Post wants to claim that not only would this accidental duplicate not have hopes, beliefs, fears, etc., it also would not have a heart, liver, brain, eyes, etc. Of course, Post is wrong about this. I agree that the physical duplicate would not necessarily have the same intentional states or those states corresponding to propositional attitudes that existed in the original being, but to say it does not have a heart, lungs, etc., when one has already claimed that it is a physical duplicate is simply to contradict oneself.

This argument by Post seems extremely strained in order to avoid a reductive analysis of the mind-body problem or the self-body relationship. He even goes so far as to argue in the following way: The reductivist is going to claim some causal relation as existing between the supervenient properties in question and their subvenient properties. Post contrives a situation in which it is clearly the case that a particular N property supervenes upon a given set of P properties but was not causally derived from those properties. Post describes the situation in this way:

> Now suppose I come to believe, perhaps as a result of being kicked in the head, that Saturn's rings contain a certain ammonia molecule. Call it "Ammon". Suppose Ammon is indeed contained in Saturn's rings, so the belief happens to be true (though I have no evidence that it is). Thus one of my belief's non-physical properties, namely truth, is determined at least in part by something to do with Ammon's physical properties. Yet there is no causal connection between my belief and Ammon. Doubt on this score can be dispelled by changing the example to make Ammon a particle in the rings of a planet outside what physicists call my 'backward light cone'; no causal signal, not even light, can reach me from Ammon. Whether my belief is true depends

not only on whether it possesses certain physical properties and causal relations, including a physical history, but also on what physical properties Ammon has, even though Ammon's having them cannot result in some causal physical relation between the belief and Ammon.[34]

Post claims that this example is another dent in the connective generalization argument by the reductivist, but also that it shows that

> our psychological attributes, such as having a particular true belief, are not determined solely by our own physical properties and causal physical relations but can depend on something so trifling and seemingly irrelevant as a single molecule in a distant planet's rings.[35]

But, why should anyone who wants to argue for a nonreductive physicalism (as Post claims he is doing in both The Faces of Existence and Metaphysics: A Contemporary Introduction) go to these lengths to argue against reductive physicalism?

First, allow me to repeat myself. Not all reductive approaches are of an ontological type ('nothing butism'). Rather, it is conceivable that the reductivism in question is of a nomological type by which the laws governing microphysical properties could be extended to the supervenient properties without the supervenient properties losing their distinctiveness.

Second, and most important, what does Post gain by loosening the supervenient-subvenient relationship? If one replaces connective generalization with some kind of determination that also does not hold in all cases of the subvenient properties, how different is this from dualism? Surely, we can agree that supervenient properties can be identical in type even though the subvenient properties may vary, e.g., in moral situations. With his exact duplicate heart and human being examples, has he not lost the whole purpose of the concept of supervenience? I believe he has. His vague and unconvincing linking of an entity's function to its history does not serve the self's supervenience upon psychological and physical properties very well when he applies the notion of history to organs per se. In regard to the question of the self, I would agree that the history (story) of the self is extremely important in respect to who the self is and, therefore, in respect to the self's identity. But this application of the term 'history' applies more appropriately to the decisions and plans generated by the individual who has a specific self than it does to the causal sequence of microparticles making up a physical organ. It would seem that he has taken the term 'history' from its proper context in order to make it do metaphorical work in a context that does not lend itself very easily nor insightfully to the metaphor. Ultimately, Post finds D1 unsatisfactory. It is less

> exclusionary than generalization accounts, but it too seems influenced by microreductive proclivities that focus on the thing's own physical properties and relations.
> What is needed is an explication according to which the physical conditions not only of x but also of things that bear no significant physical relation to x can determine nonphysical matters about x. The needed idea is that two physically possible worlds, the same as regards which physical conditions obtain in them, are also the same as regards which non-physical conditions obtain in them, even when these are not physical conditions of the same things.[36]

This possible set of relationships desired by Post issues forth in D2: 'D2 – Given any two physically possible worlds W1 and W2, if the same physical conditions obtain in both, the same nonphysical conditions obtain in both, . . .'.[37] However, Post himself hypothesizes a possible criticism to the effect that D2 is too vague in the sense that it does not indicate that it is a specific set of physical properties that determine 'a given nonphysical condition or phenomenon N'.[38] The physical properties that are supposed to be determinative in respect to the N properties could be anywhere in this world. Post does not seem impressed with this criticism. He claims that what is important is to be in possession of D2 after which the notion of 'the specific P-conditions that determine N' can be explicated:

> Merely define them as the P-conditions that form the least set that suffices to determine N. To say that they form the least such set is to say that they but no proper subset of them suffice to determine N. In this way, D2 enables us to combine specificity with the relational, historical, and holistic thinking involved in much that needs to be accounted for.[39]

This approach is truly strange. Merely to state a formal or a priori set of minimal conditions whereby P properties determine N properties can hardly count as providing the specificity of the P properties pertinent to a set of N properties in question. D2 still allows for a scattering of the "least set" of P properties. What is needed in order for one to identify specifically the relation of determination or supervenience as obtaining between a set of physical properties and a set of nonphysical properties is some kind of experiential identification of the properties in question. To allow for the possibility of P conditions being scattered in a possible world in which they determine N properties simply strains our credulity. I realize that we do live in a wondrous world and not all that is real has in fact matched with our credulity over the centuries – witness the march of natural science. Nevertheless, Post's attempt to salvage a nonreductive determination or supervenience does not square with our experience in identifying the P properties that determine a given set of N properties. And if this is correct, then D2 must give way to D1 once again. That is, if one is driven to an experiential identification of the subvenient P properties that give rise to the supervenient N properties in question, then is not the possibility of a connective generalization still in effect? I do not see how he can avoid connective generalizations if my criticism of his method of identifying the specificity of P properties relative to N properties holds.

When it comes to the question of the supervenience of the self or selfhood upon psychological and physical properties and the self's identity over time, one is going to be more concerned about subvenient properties that have a direct bearing upon the supervenient as opposed to the exceedingly improbable conditions obtaining in Post's thought-experiments, e.g., the belief in Ammon. Post describes Millikan's understanding of true beliefs as having a bearing upon survival. He then indicates that Millikan's biosemantics allows for the possibility 'that in certain cases the affairs mapped may be so distant that no causal chain connects them to the beliefs. Nor need the truth of a particular belief always play a role in explaining survival.'[40] Millikan's biosemantics is apparently consistent with a naturalistic interpretation of language and, therefore, is consistent with the physicalist's point of view. So Millikan's biosemantics affords a naturalistic view of truth that provides enough latitude for some instances of nonphysical properties being determined by physical properties that have no causal influence upon the nonphysical properties. One is reminded of Post's case of a true belief not having been causally produced by the conditions in question (the Ammon example).

But, what kind of support is afforded our understanding of the self by the notion that a supervenient property (the belief that one of Saturn's rings contains Ammon) occurring through a causal succession (being kicked in the head) that has nothing to do with the conditions that make the belief true, viz., there is an Ammon molecule in a ring of Saturn? How can such a 'straining' of the supervenient-subvenient relationship afford Post any comfort in the sense of its being a possible counter-example to reductive determination? The true belief in question was physically produced (brain cells were stimulated by a blow to the head); it was not through a causal series actually having the Ammon of Saturn's ring as its terminus in some sense that the belief was produced. Why is Post so determined on arguing his case (nonreductive physicalism) by basing it on a 'Cambridge change'?

There is a better way to call reductionism into question than through the incredible machinations devised by Post. Let us turn to Alan Garfinkel's essay 'Reductionism'. Garfinkel takes the reductionistic clause the 'such and such(1) is just such and such(2)' and puts it into an explanatory frame of reference. The point of asserting 'such and such(1) is just such and such (2)' is to frame an explanation. More accurately, reduction is a matter of one explanation replacing another. For such a replacement to be successful, however, it is necessary that the reducing explanation have the same object as the reduced explanation. 'This means that they must be about the same phenomena and also that they must construe the problematic in the same way.'[41]

Garfinkel takes issue with Oppenheim and Putnam's position as presented in their 'Unity of Science as a Working Hypothesis' that 'theory A is reducible to theory B if B explains all the observation sentences that A does'[42] on the grounds that it is not sentences that are the objects of explanation. Another problem with the Oppenheim-Putnam view is the emphasis placed on observation:

> Even if theory B explained all the observation sentences that theory A does, its status as a reduction would be in doubt unless it could also explain the mechanisms and postulated unobservables, the explaining entities, of theory A.[43]

It is Garfinkel's belief that if these two features of the Oppenheim-Putnam program are denied, then one will come up with 'a more realist notion of reduction', viz., 'theory A is reducible to theory B if theory B explains the phenomena previously the province of theory A'. [44]

At this point, however, Garfinkel moves to a critique of the belief that if one is able to generate a microexplanation of a macrostate, then the macroexplanation is dispensable. Garfinkel chooses, as an example of where both the micro and macro explanations are indispensable to the understanding of a phenomenon, the population of foxes and rabbits in a given area. When the population of foxes rises, the population of the rabbits decreases to a certain point at which the foxes are in more competition with one another, thereby causing some of the foxes to leave the area, die, etc. Subsequently, the rabbit population increases once again. But let us suppose that the fox population is at the most dangerous point for rabbits prior to the competitive point. A macroexplanation for the death of a rabbit at this time would be: 'The cause of the death of the rabbit was that the fox population was high'.[45] The microexplanation for the death of the rabbit in question would be something like: 'Rabbit r was eaten because he passed through the capture space of fox f.'[46] In Garfinkel's estimation, the microexplanation cannot deal with the question of why the rabbit was more likely to be eaten at that time than a year before. The microexplanation can tell us why the rabbit was eaten at a specific time and place (because it was in the capture space-time frame of a specific fox f), but it does not tell us that if fox f had not been present, then it would have been probable that fox g would have taken its place. Obviously, in this case, the macroexplanation takes on more importance for the rabbit than does the microexplanation because it is the macroexplanation that tells the rabbit of its high level of vulnerability because of the increased number of foxes in the area. 'The microexplanation does not tell us this and does not tell us how sensitive the outcome is to changes in the conditions. Therefore, it does not tell us what things would have to be otherwise for the rabbit not to get eaten.'[47] Garfinkel calls the high probability that the rabbit would have been eaten by another fox g if fox f had not been available 'redundant causality'.[48]

> Systems which exhibit redundant causality therefore have, for every consequent Q, a bundle of antecedents (Pi) such that:
> 1. If any one of the Pi is true, so will be Q.
> 2. If one Pi should not be the case, some other will.
> Obviously, in any system with redundant causality, citing the actual Pi that caused Q will be defective as an explanation. This will apply to many cases in which Pi is the microexplanation.[49]

Garfinkel indicates that it is understandable why the reductionist turns to a microexplanation. Obviously, if the microphenomena did not occur, the macroexplanation would be without content. Without the microphenomena, the structural fact lying behind the macroexplanation would be nonexistent and, therefore, would not provide a cause upon which the macroexplanation depends. On the other hand, 'merely citing the specific mechanism which brought about the effect does not tell us the important fact that had that particular mechanism not occurred, then some other would have, to accomplish the same end'.[50]

Garfinkel's approach to reductionism allows for a full-fledged physicalism to be maintained without forcing one to appropriate the lengths that Post takes in calling 'nothing but' reductionism into question. As Garfinkel says, 'So the fact that something materially "is" something else does not mean that we can reduce the explanations involved'.[51]

Garfinkel asserts that merely because actions have a 'neurophysiological substratum' that is not to say that the actions are explained neurophysiologically. In the Phaedo, Socrates agrees with this point:

The reason he [Socrates] gives is that the neurophysiological account ('nerves and bones and sinew'), although presumably true, does not give us an explanation (aitia) of human action. A true explanation must inevitably be in terms of reasons, not 'nerves and bond and sinew'. The latter are the necessary medium of any human action, but citing them does not suffice to explain action, because, he says, it does not explain why he does one thing (staying in jail) ratherthan another (escaping).[52]

Garfinkel believes he has support for his 'independence of explanation' concept from Putnam's belief that 'mental states cannot be reduced to their material realizations in this or that organism'.[53] The point is that the phenomenon of pain, for example, could conceivably exist in entities with different physical substrates. Thus, a functionalist point of view seems to suggest that different levels of states (mental or brain) demand different levels of explanation.

Another interesting point developed by Garfinkel is the claim that a microexplanation is inadequate if it depends upon characteristics belonging to a macroexplanation. I will not summarize Garfinkel's example in detail, but he uses the Boyle-Charles law regarding the activity of gases to defend this point. Pressure, volume, and temperature are macroproperties of a gas, and if one tries to account for their levels solely by reference to the separate states of each individual molecule, one will find oneself using a global property that really belongs to the macro level of explanation.

> There is, to be sure, a collection of individuals (the gas molecules) with an individual nature given by Newtonian mechanics, according to which they areessentially small elastic particles. But the properties of the gas, like the Boyle-Charles law, do not arise simply from this individual nature. We must make, in addition, strong assumptions about the collective possibilities of the system, assumptions which are imposed on the individual nature and do not in any sense follow from it.[54]

This point is similar to the principle to which Kathleen Lennon (*Explaining Human Action*) holds in respect to the efficacy of reduction, viz., 'There must be no explanatory work done by the reduced property which cannot be done by the reducing property'.[55] In Garfinkel's example of the behavior of gases, global properties or collective considerations operable on the macro level of explanation are not sufficiently captured by the behavior of separate and individual molecules taken non-collectively.

Having tried to make a case for a kind of supervenience that is not reductive in kind, I want to pursue further in the next chapter in what sense the self can be considered a supervenient property or set of properties. In order to do this, it is helpful to look at the notion of tropes or abstract particulars.

## Notes

[1]  Ibid., 261.
[2]  Kim, 259, quoting R. M. Hare, *The Language of Morals* (London, 1952), 145.
[3]  Jaegwon Kim, 'Supervenience as a Philosophical Concept', *Metaphilosophy* 21 (January/April 1990): 9.
[4]  D. M. Armstrong, *A Combinatorial Theory of Possibility* (Cambridge: Cambridge University Press, 1989) 103
[5]  Ibid., 103.
[6]  Kim, 'Supervenience as a Philosophical Concept', 8.
[7]  Ibid., 23.
[8]  Ibid., 22.
[9]  Ibid., 13-17.
[10]  Ibid., 13-14.
[11]  Ibid., 14.
[12]  Ibid., 14-15.
[13]  Ibid., 9.
[14]  Thomas R. Grimes, 'Supervenience, Determination, and Dependency', *Philosophical Studies* 62 (1991): 86.
[15]  Kim, 'Supervenience as a Philosophical Concept', 17.
[16]  Ibid.
[17]  Ibid., 19.
[18]  Ibid., 21.
[19]  Ibid.
[20]  John Post, *Metaphysics: A Contemporary Introduction* (New York: Paragon House, 1991), 95ff.
[21]  Ibid., 98-99.
[22]  Ibid.
[23]  John Post, *The Faces of Existence* (Ithaca, N.Y.: Cornell University Press, 1987), 182.
[24]  Post, *Metaphysics*, 103.
[25]  Ibid., 104.
[26]  Ibid., 107-108.
[27]  Ibid., 109.
[28]  Ibid., 110.

[29] Ibid.

[30] Ibid.

[31] Ibid., 111.

[32] Ibid., 111-112.

[33] Ibid., 112.

[34] Ibid., 115-116.

[35] Ibid.

[36] Ibid., 117.

[37] Ibid., 118.

[38] Ibid.

[39] Ibid.

[40] Ibid.

[41] Alan Garfinkel, 'Reductionism', *The Philosophy of Science,* ed. Richard Boyd et al (Cambridge, Mass.: The MIT Press, 1991,), 444.

[42] Ibid.

[43] Ibid., 445.

[44] Ibid.

[45] Ibid., 446.

[46] Ibid., 447.

[47] Ibid.

[48] Ibid., 448.

[49] Ibid.

[50] Ibid., 449.

[51] Ibid.

[52] Ibid., 450.

[53] Ibid.

[54] Ibid., 456-57.

[55] Kathleen Lennon, *Explaining Human Action* (LaSalle, Ill.: Open Court, 1990), 17.

# 4 The supervenient self and its relationship to tropes

**Tropes**

In this chapter, I try to make a case for understanding the ontological nature of the human self in terms of abstract particulars or tropes, a term used for abstract particulars by Donald C. Williams and, more recently, by Keith Campbell. Thus, I would like to trace, briefly, the notion of abstract particulars as understood by George Frederick Stout, an idealist writing in the first half of this century, and by Donald C. Williams who wrote on induction and metaphysical topics during the middle portion of the twentieth century. In the second section of this chapter, I will argue for an interpretation of the self as a supervenient abstract particular that is primarily based on Campbell's understanding of tropes.

If one accepts the notion that there are certain basic categories or classifications of reality, then one will also often find among the philosophers who share this belief (ontologists) those who are courageous enough (or foolhardy enough) to compose lists of these categories. Aristotle's list had ten such, and a recent ontologist, Reinhardt Grossmann, lists seven basic categories. But whether ontologists overtly generate such lists, many will include the categories of particulars and universals (or individuals and properties, or individuals and characteristics, or individuals and qualities, etc. – pairs not necessarily synonymous with the pair preceding the parentheses) on their private lists of the basic classifications of what things there are in this universe. The very real danger of even attempting a crude characterization of these two categories, universals and particulars, is to run the risk of begging the question for or against the existence of the category under consideration. For example, if I were to characterize universals as being those qualities held in common by different particulars which in turn are those entities of which qualities may be 'predicated' but are themselves not predicated of anything, then I could possibly be accused of begging the question in favor of universals being something that, in some sense, can exist apart from concrete entities because of my use of the phrase 'qualities held in common'. I might be accused of begging the question in this case because some hold that qualities 'instantiated' in several different individuals or particulars – even though appearing to be identical – are, in fact, merely similar (and, thus, not held in common) and, therefore, not 'universals' after all. Thus, such a philosopher would not allow my description of a universal to pass unchallenged. With this general caveat in mind, i.e., that even fundamental descriptions of ontological categories are open to serious philosophical question, let us take a look at the notion of abstract particulars as understood by G. F. Stout and D. C. Williams.

Stout published a very controversial article, 'The Nature of Universals and Propositions', in 1921-22 in the *Proceedings of the British Academy*. With the caveat mentioned above well in mind, let me simply characterize Stout's position on universals as being one which denies that universals exist as identities. Rather,

> [a] character characterizing a concrete thing or individual is as particular as the thing or individual which it characterizes. Of two billiard balls, each has its own particular roundness separate and distinct from that of the other, just as the billiard balls themselves are distinct and separate. . . . What then do we mean when we say, for instance, that roundness is a character common to all billiard balls? I answer that the phrase 'common character' is elliptical. It really signifies a certain general kind or class of characters. To say that particular things share in the common character is to say that each of them has a character which is a particular instance of this kind or class of characters.[1]

For Stout, a substance is nothing apart from its qualities. He agrees that there are concrete things, but these things are complex unities of characters or qualities.

In turn, these characters are particulars but not concrete particulars.

> A substance is a complex unity of an altogether ultimate and peculiar type, including within it all characters truly predicable of it. To be truly predicable of it is to be contained within it. The distinctive unity of such a complex is *concreteness*. Characters of concrete things are

particular, but not concrete. What is concrete is the whole in which they coalesce with each other. [2]

How does Stout respond to the advocates of the 'singleness of character' (those who believe that a quality such as 'redness' is indivisible and at the same time can be in two or more different spatial or temporal locales)? Taking the case of two billiard balls, each seemingly exemplifying one and the same color, Stout would maintain that since each billiard ball is spatially discrete from the other, then what would appear to be an absolutely identical color in each case cannot be such. He would dispute the notion that a singular term can be accurately applied to the color(s); rather, even though both balls have a cream color, 'cream' in this case is used as a general term. For Stout, not only are the two billiard balls members of the subclass of cream colored things which in turn is a member of the general class of colored things, but 'creamness' is a subclass contained within the class of 'color'. [3]

Stout claims that he avoids being classified as a nominalist on the basis that he does not depend upon 'resemblance' as the relation that determines the class in question. The problem with nominalism is that

> [t]he nominalist entirely fails to show how we can think of a class or kind as a whole without setting out before our mind each one of its members or instances so as to discern relations of similarity between them. Yet he cannot help tacitly assuming that this is not required for our apprehension of the class as a whole. [4]

But if it is not resemblance that allows one to group tropes together under common terms such as 'red', 'hard', etc., and, of course, if it cannot be identity that allows such grouping because that explanation would vitiate the rationale for tropes in the first place, then what is it? Stout, as indicated above, relies upon the class membership of tropes to provide the rationale for using general terms. He does not dispense with the notion of resemblance entirely in this matter, but he claims that it is a relation holding between terms in virtue of their membership in the same class. He speaks of classes as having a 'distributive unity' that is basic or fundamental – 'the distributive unity of a class or kind is an ultimate and unanalysable type of unity'. [5]

> How then, it may be asked, are relations of resemblance connected with the distributive unity of a class or kind? My own view is briefly as follows. A relation considered as subsisting between terms presupposes some complex unity within which both terms and relations fall. This complex unity is the *fundamentum relationis*. For example, a relation of

'above and below' as subsisting between *a* and *b* and the special relation between them. In like manner, resemblance presupposes a complex unity of the peculiar type which I call the distributive unity of a class.[6]

Without going into a long discussion on the dangers of asserting that the members of a class determine a class (not that Stout maintains this particular point) nor engaging in a discussion of how some classes can have members with nothing in common and, at the same time, how the concept of class often serves sortal purposes, it still seems to me that Stout must wrestle with the question of how one can go about identifying a class of tropes without using the similarity of the members as the distinguishing mark of the class in question. Simply to assert that there is 'complex unity' (Stout's 'distributive unity' of a class) which serves as the determiner of a term's class membership seems extremely obscure, especially if some sets (equatable to classes in some cases)[7] are simply arbitrary collections of objects and, on the other hand, other classes serve as classification concepts. How can one determine when 'distributive unity' is operating, and when it is not?

Now, I am well aware that one should not necessarily assume that a distinguishing characteristic of something should be treated as the cause or origination of that bearing the characteristic. This point makes eminently good sense in respect to a concrete particular bearing a certain characteristic. But is a class (which does, after all, seem to be an abstraction) sufficiently similar to a concrete particular so that one should never ascribe the origination of the class to the similarity of properties by which one identifies the class in question? I am arguing, of course, that the notion of distributive unity is too obscure to provide much insight into how similar but different tropes can be grouped under common terms. In fact, one must wonder if Stout is not depending upon the concept of 'identity' under another name?

Let me mention another problem that was raised by G. E. Moore. Moore's most telling criticism of Stout's understanding of characteristics occurs in respect to Stout's position that the spatial location of concrete particulars, e.g., two billiard balls, is known by one's knowing the different spatial locations of the characteristics constituting the concrete particulars.[8] Further, Stout then assumes that the spatial distinction existing between the characteristics of the two billiard balls is due to the fact that the characteristics are different even though they may appear to be identical. Thus, the cream color of the one billiard ball is different from the cream color of the second billiard ball even though there is no obvious difference in the hue, saturation, or brightness of the two balls. Moore denies that merely because two characteristics have different spatial locations, one has to assert that the characteristics are not identical. He agrees that a concrete particular (thing) cannot be in two different spatial locations at one and the same time, but concrete things are not characteristics:

> But when we speak of two qualities as "locally separate" we seem to me to be using the phrase in an entirely different sense. All that we mean, or can mean, by it, is, I think, that the first belongs to a concrete thing which is locally separate (in our first sense) from a concrete thing to which the second belongs. And with *this* sense of 'locally separate', it seems to me perfectly obvious that a quality can be 'locally separate' from itself: one and the same quality *can* be in two different places at the same time. Indeed, to deny that it can be is simply to beg the original question at issue. For if to say 'the specific color of A is locally separate from the specific color of B' merely *means* that the specific color of A belongs to a concrete thing which is locally separate from a concrete thing to which the specific color of B belongs, it follows that the specific color of A *can* be 'locally separate' from itself, provided only it is true that the specific color of A *can* belong to each of two concrete things. . . . For I maintain that the same indivisible quality can really *be* locally or temporally separate; maintaining that all this means is that it can really belong to both of two concrete things or events which are, in the fundamental sense appropriate to concrete things or events, locally or temporally separate.[9]

Obviously, Moore is saying that the 'behavior' of concrete things should not serve as the model for the 'behavior' of qualities or characteristics.

Panayot Butchvarov asserts that there is something of value on both sides of the issue. On Stout's side, it does appear to be the case that qualities can be found in different spatial locations:

> Moore, on the other hand, argued that qualities do not, strictly speaking, have location in space; to say that a quality has a certain location is only to say that it is exemplified by an individual thing that has that location.[10]

At the same time, Butchvarov believes that Moore's helpful contribution to this discussion is his contention that qualities are universals, i.e., that a given quality, even though located in different places, is still one and the same (identical) quality:

> A quality may have spatial location and, moreover, be located wherever it is exemplified, but its location may be *multiple*, namely at all places where the diverse individual things exemplifying it are located. Indeed,

*individual things* cannot have multiple spatial location at the same time. But why should we suppose that this is true also of their qualities? [11]

So Butchvarov agrees with Moore's contention that qualities or characteristics need not demonstrate the same kind of 'behavior' manifested by concrete particulars or concrete things in respect to spatial (and I suspect temporal as well) location.

If we were to engage in an adequate exposition of why Butchvarov believes that identity in respect to qualities is basic as opposed to resemblance, it would be necessary to indicate at quite some length the distinction that Butchvarov makes between 'objects' and 'entities' – a distinction given impetus by Frege's 'sense' and 'nominatum' discussion.[12] But, we can say this much: that for Butchvarov identity is a primitive concept – a concept that determines other concepts:

> One may recognize that the color or shape or feel or smell of an object is the same as the color or shape or feel or smell of another object without possessing the appropriate specific (e.g., 'red') or even generic (e.g., 'color') concept. And small children (perhaps also some animals) are quite capable of judging whether something is the same as something else (e.g., whether a certain trinket is *his*, whether it is the one *he* found), even if possessing no relevant sortal concepts and no relevant linguistic competence. Such identity judgments are the obvious first and absolutely necessary step in the very acquisition of any appropriate sortal concept.[13]

Besides this affirmative statement supporting identity, Butchvarov also has a negative statement to make about resemblance serving as a primitive concept in the place of identity. In his analysis of resemblance, Butchvarov does not depend upon Russell's repudiation of nominalism's dependence on resemblance. Russell tried to show that in order for nominalism to avoid an infinite regress in resemblances (resemblances between qualities demand resemblances between the resemblances of the qualities, etc.), it would be necessary for nominalism to claim resemblance as a universal. But to do so is to open the door for the existence of universals and, therefore, why stop at one universal? Without indicating the steps of his argument, we can say that Butchvarov concludes that the alleged infinite regress is not a vicious one. Instead, Butchvarov believes that resemblance statements are either logically incomplete or surreptitiously dependent upon the concept of universals. Again, space forestalls a complete account of Butchvarov's argument, but an example of the logically incomplete nature of resemblance statements is given in the following passage:

Initially, the Resemblance Theory may be taken as claiming simply that a case of the recurrence of qualities is an ordinary dyadic relational fact, adequately describable in statements of the form R(x,y), e.g., 'The color of this page resembles the color of the next page'. But this claim is easily seen to be false. The fact is that resemblance statements of that form are logically incomplete (even though the contexts in which they are made often disguise this fact), in the precise sense that as they stand they have no determinate truth-value, that there are no sufficient or necessary conditions for their truth. For example, for the color of this page and the color of the next page to resemble each other, must they resemble exactly, or almost exactly, or just in that both are white, or just in that both are colors, rather than say a color and a shape, or perhaps even just in that both are qualities, rather than say a quality and individual thing?[14]

As indicated, the preceding passage is just a portion of Butchvarov's account of the deficiency of resemblance statements, but I think it is the most important of his arguments against resemblance because it speaks directly against the notion that resemblance is the primitive concept in the identification of the recurrence of qualities. This argument coupled with his treatment of identity as a primitive concept seems to be conclusive, and this outcome would be unfortunate for my position inasmuch as I argue that the self is a supervenient abstract particular in the next section of this chapter.

So, what I want to do at this point is to turn Butchvarov's argument around somewhat so that even if the outcome in favor of resemblance is not conclusive, it will be plausible to a degree. Returning to the Stout-Moore controversy, let us notice that neither Moore nor Butchvarov will accept the notion that the 'behavior' of concrete things in respect to spatial location must serve as the paradigm for the 'behavior' of characteristics or qualities. Even though different spatial locations for two concrete things indicate that they are two discrete and different concrete things, the same situation does not necessarily hold for qualities. For Butchvarov, one and the same quality may, in fact, exist in two different locations.

However, what other paradigm do we have available for distinguishing one object (used in a broad philosophical sense) from another if it is not by observing what constitutes the distinction between one concrete particular (thing) from another – especially if the object(s) in question are intimately tied to concrete particulars? Stout might have been in error in asserting that the different spatial locations of qualities belonging to the same class or subclass indicate that they are not identical, and Butchvarov's statement – 'Indeed, *individual things* cannot have multiple spatial location at the same time. But why should we suppose that this is true also of their qualities?' – is well-taken. But, then, maybe it is the case that the different spatial locations of qualities belonging to the same class is the index of their difference! The point is: Neither Stout nor Butchvarov have enough evidence relative to the spatial location of qualities and concrete particulars to make an ontological claim one way or the other as to whether qualities are universals or abstract particulars.

Thus, whether one accepts qualities as being universals or as being abstract particulars will depend upon the supporting arguments for identity in the one case and for resemblance on the other. Much of the strength of Butchvarov's argument for identity turns upon his treating it as a primitive concept. However, Donald Cary Williams in a posthumously published article (published in 1986 but written about 1959) takes the same tack with resemblance:

> At this stage we conjecture that we are much less likely to explain similarity as due to the presence of a common or general constituent than to explain the notion of a common or general constituent as somehow a resultant of similarity – a procedure to which, in fact, I was committed as soon as I laid it down that similarity is an irreducible and categorical element.[15]

Now, when in the treatment of the very similar colors of two different lollipops one is inclined to say of this trope A (the color of lollipop x) that it is lemon yellow and that this trope B (the color of lollipop y) is also lemon yellow, one is tempted to avoid the apparent inconsistency of two different objects being one and the same thing by declaring that lemon yellow is a universal that is held in common by two different particulars, viz., the lollipops. And trope-theory is, therefore, destroyed. But this move is unnecessary according to Williams.[16] Rather, the lemon yellow that is A is still different from the lemon yellow that is B even though both are very much alike. But in applying terms to our experiences there is a 'weaker' kind of 'identity conditions' used for 'kinds' as opposed to 'stronger' identity conditions that are in place for particulars:

> That universals are not made nor discovered but are, as it were, 'acknowledged' by a relaxation of identity conditions of thought and language, will become more attractive as we notice, for example, that similar relaxations occur in our treatment of ordinary proper names of concrete particulars, especially in the common idiom which, innocent of the notion of temporal parts of a thing, finds the whole enduring object, a man or a stone, in each momentary stage of its history. For

here and now, we say, *is* the person called 'John', not just part but all of him, and now again here is the same 'John', all present at another instant, though in strict ontology the 'John' of today is a batch of being as discrete from the 'John' of yesterday as he is from the moon. The relaxation of conditions which acknowledges universals, however, and which I shall call 'generizing' (because 'generalizing' is commonly used not for conceiving universals but for conceiving or asserting laws), is much more firmly seated in the facts of language and its object than any other I know.[17]

Thus, it is conceivable that resemblance or similarity is a primitive concept, and identity can be understood as a derivative of the use of language in application to similar but different tropes and/or to groupings of tropes (concrete particulars). Williams wants to make it clear, however, that he is not asserting that language creates reality. Tropes and groupings of tropes constitute reality:

> It is by a twist of language that we designate them [universals], it is true, singly or in troops, but it is only by twists of language that we designate anything, and none of these twists creates its own designatum.[18]

A possible reply that Butchvarov may make to Williams' notion that there is a relaxation of identity conditions in the application of general terms to qualities (and, thus, 'qualities' become 'universals') is found in Butchvarov's distinction between words and concepts. A concept, for Butchvarov, 'is essentially a principle of classification'.[19] And, thus,

> [i]f there are cases in which the application of the word "blue" is indeterminate, this shows that there is no one concept expressed by the word, not that there is an indeterminate concept. Unlike a word, a concept must either clearly apply to a given thing or fail to belong to it, even though the corresponding predicate may, in some cases, neither clearly apply nor clearly fail to apply. We must not lose sight of the enormous difference between language, on one hand, and thought and the world, on the other.[20]

Butchvarov believes that the basis for the use of sortal concepts is, in fact, the human's ability to apply the primitive concept of identity to recurring qualities.[21] Ignoring for the moment Butchvarov's belief that our use or application of concepts to things is as precise as he claims, we must ask the question whether similarity or resemblance cannot serve in a sufficiently determinate way as the basis for our use of sortal concepts rather than identity. If I see a red ball at location l(1) and another red ball at location l(2) could I not say that ball(1) is *very much like* ball(2) in terms of color instead of asserting or even believing that red(1) is identical to red(2)? I doubt that many would deny that this linguistic and/or belief response is possible and, therefore, the classification of qualities is possible on a resemblance theory approach as well as an identity theory approach. The choice of one approach over the other has to be based on arguments other than the phenomenological one just described. And, now, let us return to a very strong argument mounted by identity theorists such as Butchvarov.

In a long passage quoted above, Butchvarov indicates that if resemblance theory is interpreted as promoting the notion that a recurrence of qualities is to be treated as a 'dyadic relational fact', as represented in a statement such as 'The color of this page resembles the color of the next page', then this interpretation is wrong because such statements are logically incomplete. There are insufficient conditions for determining the truth-values of such sentences. An attempt to provide a reference to such conditions, however, requires one to use the very notion that resemblance theory is understood to repudiate, viz., a universal (understood in terms of identity). In order to specify the kind of resemblance (in this case, ruling out a shape or a *specific* color, etc.) in use in regard to a dyadic comparison, one must specify the respect in which the resemblance is being used. Unfortunately for resemblance theory, that will necessitate reference to a universal (identity type), and, therefore, as Butchvarov says,

> Such resemblance statements [those including the *respect* in which the resemblance comparison is being made] are, of course, logically coherent and complete. But they fail to be genuine, clear alternatives to the corresponding identity statements. For are they not merely verbose rewordings of '*a* and *b* are the same color'? (*a* and *b*, we must not forget, are the colors of the two pages, not the pages themselves.)[22]

D. W. Hamlyn provides very strong support for Butchvarov's position in his summary of the position taken by such thinkers as D. M. Armstrong, Arthur Pap, and Frank Jackson toward this issue:

> In sum, it does not seem possible to eliminate the reference to respects in *all* cases where it is proposed to do without reference to universals by analysing propositions which apparently make such a reference in terms of particular things and their similarity. Hence there will certainly be as many universals as are generated by such cases. If we have to have so many [as opposed to the nominalist settling for one, viz., resemblance] there seems little point in being abstemious

beyond that, although the questions that I mentioned earlier as to whether there are any limits on them still remain.[23]

But I contend that the inevitable reference to universals (again, of an identity sort) seemingly performed by the resemblance theorist does not have to depend upon identity as a primitive concept.

The resemblance theorist (and, thus, trope theorists) do not deny the use of general terms. Thus, there must be some mechanism in place for the application of such terms. Let us suppose along with Butchvarov that concepts are the classificatory principles that 'thought' must use in respect to the 'recurrence of qualities'. The application of general terms to objects, then, is performed accurately if the relevant concepts are functioning properly (*ceteris paribus*). Earlier, it was noted that for Butchvarov the application of terms may be indeterminate, but the application of concepts is not. Either a given concept applies to the object in question, or it does not.

But it would appear that in this approach concepts are determinative of universals; otherwise how can one explain such precision of application to objects? It appears to be the case that only if concepts are free from the vagaries of the subject's idiosyncratic mental operations can such precision be attained. However, the notion that concepts are determinative of universals is a moot point. Such a position on the relation of concepts might even suggest a kind of idealism, e.g., G. E. Moore in his earliest period. On the other hand, if such freedom can be attained, in what sense then are concepts different from propositional functions or universals themselves? There is no doubt that Butchvarov must deal with the first of these alternatives because he claims in no uncertain terms that it is a 'nonintentional' consciousness that is involved in the application of a concept to an entity:

> H. H. Price defined a concept as a capacity for recognition. Agreeing with his view that recognition is the most fundamental case in which a concept is actualized, I should rather say that a concept is a capacity for nonintentional consciousness of a certain entity, the occurrence of which consciousness is a necessary condition for the occurrence of recognition, the other necessary condition being the occurrence of intentional consciousness, a singling out, of the object that is recognized as being that entity.[24]

Without engaging in an exposition of either Butchvarov's notion of nonintentional consciousness in distinction to intentional consciousness and his technical distinction between entity and object, I believe that I can still make my point.[25] If concepts are intimately involved *as a capacity* for a subject's consciousness of entities (nonintentional) and also in the singling out of 'objects'(a technical term used by Butchvarov that could be understood as having its roots in Frege's notion of 'sense' or 'mode of presentation') pertaining to that entity (intentional consciousness), might they not be, as capacities, 'tainted' with the peculiar psychological associations of the subject using the concepts? Or, with the subject's idiosyncratic perspective? Surely, this subjectivizing of concepts must be recognized as a possibility, and if so, then on what basis can one be sure that the universals instantiated by an entity exist precisely in the same way that the subject subsumes them under his/her concepts? I do not think that even though this is an epistemological question it can be brushed aside on the grounds that we are dealing with ontological matters. Once consciousness is brought into play in respect to concepts, the question of the identification of pristine universals can be raised. If the concepts could conceivably be 'fuzzy', might not the universals also be 'fuzzy', thereby lending themselves to recognition (and reidentification) through resemblance rather than through identity? It is at least a reasonable question. Again, one of the points of the preceding argument is the attempt to generate some measure of plausibility for treating resemblance as a primitive concept.

Hamlyn's description of the position of those using the 'specifiable in some respect' argument is encapsulated in the following statement: 'Resemblance is always resemblance in some respect, and the attempt to spell out the respects will entail recognition of the universals corresponding to them.'[26] But, this argument is not totally conclusive against the trope theorist because the members of the class of qualities (which class then bears a name which has been treated as a 'universal') in question are identified through comparison based on *resemblance and not identity*. And, then, a general term is used to refer to the members of the class – the very same term time and again giving rise to the notion that the same term implies the same thing. Or, an identical term implies an identical quality. Or, one can put it as Williams did. In respect to qualities, there is a relaxation of the identity standards in the application of terms. Thus, the 'specifiable in some respect' argument is not nearly as telling when resemblance is treated as a primitive concept.

### The supervenient self as a trope

As we proceed in this section, it will become clear that the self must be treated as a trope. The self is an abstract entity, but as such it could be considered either as a universal or as a trope. I will argue that it is best considered as a particular (and therefore as a trope) inasmuch as it manifests features of uniqueness.

However, I do not want to identify the self with the concept of the ego because even if there were such an entity, it cannot be experienced by another person. The same reason applies to identifying the self with consciousness and/or self-constituting consciousness. The self, as I understand it, must be available to the experience of the human individual bearing the self and to other persons as well. As I have indicated, the concept of the person or self cannot be reduced either to physical qualities or to psychological properties taken separately because neither provides an adequate basis for the application of the concept of personal identity to the person or self, so much so that for some thinkers such as Parfit, the Humean denial of personal identity is the appropriate position to take on the matter. Even so, we refuse to give up the notion of personal identity because from the third person point of view it is the basis for moral evaluation, prediction of human behavior, and legal practice. And from the first person point of view, personal identity is corroborated by our awareness of our 'taking the past into consideration–in our decision making in the present–relative to our desire to affect the future'. This kind of personal orientation to time which involves a sense of 'something' (self or person) enduring through time demands our belief in personal identity for this orientation to make any sense. Of course, this whole program of reasons why the notion of personal identity is essential to human individuals could be simply rejected for the reason that eliminative materialism is true and nothing intentional exists after all. However, I will try to address the eliminative materialist's objections to intentional states in my analysis of Lennon and Dretske's approaches to intentionality and behavior in Chapter V.

The question before us, then, is: How can the self be understood as a supervenient quality? As a supervenient quality, it would have to depend upon the physical and psychological (meant in the broad sense) qualities of the human individual in question. Just as the moral quality of badness supervenes upon the conditions of the interior of a bank building – a person with a smoking gun is grabbing a bag of money from a teller, another teller is on the floor with blood pouring from a head wound, and at least one person is conscious of the preceding physical conditions – so too would the self supervene upon conditions such as a grouping of bodily qualities (height, brain states, color of eyes, color of skin, etc.), psychological qualities (memories, consciousness at the moment, intentions, intentional states, etc.) and social institutions or arrangements. (This last grouping of subvenient properties will be treated in C. VI.) The supervenient quality of the self is not given to us in a perceptual manner devoted specifically to the self any more than the supervenient quality of badness is given to us in a perceptual manner devoted specifically to the case of badness discerned in the bank robbery illustration. We cannot 'locate' the self in the same manner as one locates an individual's brain states or skin color. Yet, just as an individual's psychological qualities must be attached or connected to a specific grouping of physical qualities, so must the quality of the self be 'connected' to a specific grouping of physical and psychological qualities. Supervenient qualities must be 'instantiated' in some sense. Otherwise, freely floating supervenient qualities would be possible, and I have already rejected this possibility in my criticism of Post's attempt to use D(2) in order to ground mental events upon physical events and still have some latitude for 'relational, historical, and holistic thinking'.[27]

But what instantiates the quality of selfhood? Is it not enough merely to say that a specific grouping of physical and psychological qualities denominated as human individual 'x' is the subvenient base for self 'x'? I do not have any difficulty with the thrust of this question because on a superficial level I have no difficulty in simply accepting the thesis that it is qualities and only qualities that constitute reality. However, on a deeper level an exposition of this belief about the nature of reality is demanded in the face of those who normally think of basic reality in a more 'substantial' way (this term can be understood in two senses and I mean it in both).

I refer those who might believe that it is necessary that a quality be instantiated in a material substance to Panayot Butchvarov's analysis of the problems associated with this belief.[28] If one is to say that an individual thing (that has physical qualities and possibly non-physical qualities) is to be understood as having matter in its composition, then one of two things can happen as one attempts to conduct an analysis of this matter. One can either end up in an infinite regress as the analysis moves from level to level of types of matter (flesh and bones to protoplasm to molecules, etc.) or to an ultimate, a prime matter. Neither alternative affords an identifiable particular relative to the individual thing in question. Why? Because the first alternative does not provide an ultimate stopping place, and the second alternative, which does do that, does not provide a 'hook' upon which to hang the specificity of the individual thing in question for the reason that ultimate matter does not have an 'essence of its own, [and] is by definition characterless'.[29] If the individual thing is to have its individuality based on a material substance, then there must be something specifically the case (the thing's essence if you will) that is provided to the individual thing by its material substance that allows the individual thing to be identified over time:

> To identify it through time and thus be able to think of it as an entity requires the identification of its proximate matter through at least brief intervals of time, even if the substance need not consist of the same matter throughout its existence. Yet no identification of the proximate matter of a substance is possible, either because such an identification would involve the completion of an infinite process or because the matter on which the ultimate identification of any proximate matter

51

would depend is itself in principle unidentifiable. The supposition that there is content to the distinction between the ultimate matter of a substance remaining numerically the same through an interval of time and its being replaced by 'another' ultimate matter is obviously absurd. Therefore, given the dependence of the identity of a material substance through time on the identity of at least some of its matter, through at least some intervals of time, it follows that no identification of material substances through time is possible. [30]

Butchvarov generates another criticism as well, viz., that even if matter were to be claimed as that which provides stability to the individual thing over time, the claim would suffer from the findings of contemporary physics, in which it is clear that matter at any level is always changing. Thus, how could matter be the source of the reidentification of an individual thing over time?[31] (Notice that this observation applies negatively to any attempt to ground personal identity upon the material nature of the human individual.) Butchvarov indicates that the modern philosophers led by Hume were correct in denying that the very notion of material substance was intelligible because

> we cannot even imagine what it would be to perceive prime matter, the ultimate formless substrate. We can perceive the surfaces of what are supposed to be material substances and thus, in a sense not compatible with the Aristotelian notion of prime matter, the boundaries of their prime matter. But we cannot perceive the matter itself, as such. . . . And, of course, even if there are entities of which we can have only a purely intellectual, not perceptual, awareness, matter can hardly be supposed to be such an entity.[32]

What, then, is Butchvarov's position on that which constitutes an individual thing if it is not a combination of a material substance and qualities?

Using the notion of a 'metaphysics of qualities', he argues for an individual thing being a 'cluster' of qualities – qualities that are universals. We will delay indicating how Butchvarov explains what provides for the clustering of qualities so that an individual thing is constituted. What I want to do at this point is to return to the notion of the self as a supervenient particular and engage in a discussion with Butchvarov's approach to realism in ethics because his approach generates a possible challenge to the interpretation of the self as a supervenient property.

On what does the challenge turn? I have several times indicated that the supervenience of the self has an analogue in the supervenience of moral qualities upon natural conditions. But Butchvarov denies that goodness is a supervenient quality. If his reasons for denying goodness as a supervenient property hold up, then I have lost an analogical support for treating the self as a supervenient property. This does not establish in itself, however, that the self is not a supervenient property. Allow me to indicate the general position Butchvarov holds in respect to the nature of goodness without providing his rationale for the position. In his recent works, 'Realism in Ethics' and *Skepticism in Ethics*, Butchvarov treats goodness as a generic property that can apply to more 'specific' (used in the sense of 'species') abstract entities ('properties') such as pleasure, happiness, health, etc. that in turn can be applied to (or instantiated in) concrete entities (which I suspect can include complicated natural conditions such as my bank robbery illustrates as well as singular terms). In his defense of this position on goodness as a generic property having as its analogue the genus of the genus-species relation, Butchvarov makes a passing reference to the 'mysterious' nature of supervenience:

> If we understood goodness in this way, we would find the existence of such a property far less questionable. The property would be no more mysterious, queer, or nonnatural than its species. And we would achieve clear understanding of what might be meant by 'good-making' properties. Instead of being puzzled by the nature of such a mysterious relation of 'making' (or its converse, 'being consequential upon' or 'supervening upon'), we would be guided by the paradigm of the relationship of the specific (phenomenal) colors to the genus color.[33]

The accusation of something (in this case a relation) being mysterious is a serious one because we all know that it is all too easy for a conversant to appeal to such in order to avoid the hard issue or process of continuing to probe for the How? or the Why? of a set of conditions. For example, many of us feel uneasy when in the question of theodicy, the defender of a good God in the face of evil appeals to an eschatological verification of God's goodness. Until then it's a mystery, says the defender.

In the case of supervenience, however, its 'mysterious' nature may simply be a matter of being a given – an ultimate given. One should be cautious in labeling the recurring relationship existing between one set of distinct qualities or properties and another set as being one of supervenience because a 'scientific' explanation of the relation may be possible some day. A too-ready reliance upon supervenience may shut down an investigation into the situation. This may be part of the fear on the part of those who reject the use of the notion of supervenience in respect to the mind-body problem. To say that the mental supervenes upon the body (brain) may call up memories of the Aristotelian explanation of a falling stone – it seeks its proper place near the center of the earth – a conversation stopper if ever there was one.

After all, who knows? Someday, neurophysiology may be able to explain satisfactorily how sense contents or qualia, consciousness, intentionality, propositional attitudes, etc., are all absolutely identical to (and not merely dependent upon) precisely identifiable neurotransmitters crossing precisely identifiable synapses, etc., and, therefore, we really do not have mental events after all. Given this enlightened view, how many of us would want to be classified with the Cardinal Bellarmines of this world? One can see that the charge of mysteriousness against supervenience would be appropriate from a reductivist point of view.

Strangely, however, the very same charge has been used in what may be considered an affirmative manner (by a nonreductivist) in respect to the problem of the relationship of consciousness to the brain. Owen Flanagan in his work *Consciousness Reconsidered* has identified several main approaches to the consciousness-brain problem, one of which he calls the 'new mysterianism'. The 'old mysterians' were those thinkers who believed in a dualism of consciousness and body and that consciousness could not be explained in natural terms because it was nonnatural in kind. However, Flanagan has identified the new mysterians as nondualistic and naturalistic in their approach to this problem. He selects Colin McGinn's position as described in McGinn's article 'Can We Solve the Mind-Body Problem?' as representative of this approach. McGinn's position is described by Flanagan in the following way:

> McGinn thinks that there is some natural property or set of properties P that accounts for consciousness. Consciousness comes with our kind of brain. It supervenes on neural activity in our kind of brain.
> McGinn simply thinks that it is in principle impossible for us to comprehend P. (McGinn is somewhat unclear whether it is P that we cannot understand or *how* it is that P accounts for consciousness or makes the existence of consciousness 'intelligible'.) What natural property P causes certain neural events to be consciously experienced by realizing these very conscious states is closed to us.[34]

Did I say this could be taken as an affirmative approach by a nonreductivist? The fact is that from this description we cannot tell whether McGinn is a reductivist or not. Yet his view of the consciousness-body problem could be held by either a reductive or nonreductive naturalist. Flanagan points out that there are limits to investigations in the physical realm as reflected, for example by Heisenberg's Principle of Uncertainty. For his part, Flanagan as a naturalist rejects the new mysterian approach and believes that it is possible for us to gain more information about the relation between consciousness and the body.

Regardless of how one interprets the charge of mystery, if there actually is the kind of supervenience that is being defended and used in this work, viz., a nonreductive supervenience, then it would be inappropriate to dismiss it out of hand. Of course, it has to be defended with reasons, and I attempted that with the exposition of Post's work. One must be careful of simply assuming that the reductivists have the last word on a proper interpretation of basic reality. I am not saying that Butchvarov is a reductivist, nor am I saying that the way I have interpreted the implications of the term 'mysterious' is the way Butchvarov would interpret them. But, given no other indication of the intended meaning of 'mysterious', it could be used against supervenience as indicated. I am also not necessarily arguing for McGinn's position, even though I tend to have sympathy for it. I am not declaring one way or another on the question of whether consciousness is identical to brain states. What I want to claim is that the self is a supervenient trope, and as I have said before, the self is not identical to self-consciousness nor to consciousness nor to self-constituting consciousness nor the ego, etc. It is rather a trope that is discerned both by the human individual bearing the self and other persons having contact with the human individual in question. The self supervenes upon an innumerable quantity of physical and psychological properties belonging to the human individual in question. However, let us look at another problem that Butchvarov has with the concept of supervenience.

Butchvarov asserts in *Skepticism in Ethics*, within the context of his identification of a variety of types of skepticism in respect to moral qualities being real, that supervenience, used in respect to the identification of goodness as dependent or related to nonmoral properties, is merely a *formal* relation with no explanatory power. Butchvarov makes this claim within the narrower context of rejecting 'phenomenological skepticism'. This kind of skepticism relative to moral qualities refers to the Humean denial that when one experiences an action with moral implications, one senses the moral quality assigned to the action. In an act of murder, where is the quality of badness associated with the act? Butchvarov calls into question the Moorean notion that one is conscious of the moral quality supervening on the situation:

> Surely, the truth is that goodness is not given to consciousness in the simple and unquestionable way in which a specific shade of yellow, or a thrill of pleasure or a pang of pain, is given. And the further claim ordinarily made that goodness is necessarily given to consciousness as mysteriously supervening on some other and indeed categorially different, yet equally specific or determinate, property or properties only compounds the phenomenological absurdity. (We must not imagine that we achieve understanding

through a purely formal definition of supervenience such as the following: [Butchvarov quotes Chisholm's definition of supervenience found in *The Foundations of Knowing*.] 'a normative property G 'supervenes on' a nonnormative property H, provided only: H is necessarily such that whatever has it has G, but not necessarily such that whoever attributes it attributes G.') Formal definitions seldom produce understanding.[35]

My problem is not with the term 'mysteriously' that reappears in this passage; I have responded above to this charge. Rather, I am troubled by Butchvarov's dismissal of supervenience in terms of being merely a formal definition. Let me be fair to Butchvarov. He is not the only philosopher with very fine credentials who seems to take this attitude toward the notion of supervenience. Keith Campbell also manifests this attitude in passing in a defense of resemblance from the charge that resemblance, when used as the basic relation by which particularism dismisses universals, is guilty of an infinite regress. I do not want to engage in summarizing Campbell's position on resemblance's regress being nonvicious; I just want to indicate what appears to be a common attitude toward supervenience in metaphysical circles. He says,

> And I take it as a *cardinal principle* [my emphasis] in ontology that *supervenient 'additions' to ontology are pseudo-additions* [Campbell's emphasis]. No new being is involved. In the Creation metaphor, to bring supervenients into being calls for no separate and additional act on God's part.[36]

It would appear, then, that supervenience is an empty notion once we combine the positions of the reductivists in respect to supervenience (such as Kim) and that of certain metaphysicians. As far as the former position is concerned, I dealt with it in a preceding chapter. Allow me now to address the latter.

If Campbell is correct that ontology does not recognize a 'supervenient being' as being a 'real' addition to the ontological assay of a situation (and I am assuming that this represents Butchvarov's position fairly in his charges that supervenience is merely formal), does this mean that a 'cluster of qualities' (using Butchvarov's terminology) or a 'compresence of tropes' (using Campbell's terminology) cannot be experienced in a way different from the qualities or tropes taken separately? I suspect not. An analogous situation would be the smoothness of grains of sand taken collectively as they are poured over one's leg at the beach as opposed to that uncomfortable roughness of a single grain of sand caught between one's waistband and skin.

Simply because supervenience can be defined and is not an ultimate metaphysical category does not mean that it does not have phenomenological power.

The door is closed to Butchvarov if he were to make the claim that supervenience is merely mental. (I am not saying that he does make this claim. Let us simply follow out this possible move.) In his analysis of phenomenological skepticism's rejection of the possibility that goodness as a property is given to consciousness, Butchvarov defends the givenness of goodness to one's consciousness, that is, its reality, even though it must be one level of abstraction beyond that of those goods he denominates as abstract entities (pleasure, happiness, etc.). Thus, apparently a thing being 'abstract' does not negate the thing's reality. I would assume this would hold in respect to the notion of supervenience as well.

Further, appealing to a Sartrean interpretation of consciousness, Butchvarov argues that to assume that consciousness has contents such as representations or images or mental pictures, etc., is simply not an accurate portrayal of the nature of consciousness. He approves of Sartre's understanding of consciousness as having as its direct objects objects in the world itself. Butchvarov quotes with approval the following statement made by Sartre in *Being and Nothingness*:

> The first procedure of philosophy ought to be to expel things from consciousness and to reestablish its true connection with the world, to know that consciousness is a positional consciousness *of* the world. All consciousness is positional in that it transcends itself in order to reach an object, and it exhausts itself in this same positing.[37]

Given this interpretation of consciousness, Butchvarov with appropriate epistemological qualifications does not believe that it is impossible to accept the notion of a moral consciousness to which moral qualities are given – not in the sense of being images, representations, little pictures but in the sense of being directly given:

> To morally approve of something, we must say, can only be to be conscious of it as moral, to be conscious of its moral goodness, even if this were illusory. Ethical consciousness must be consciousness of certain objective values, of certain properties of objects, even if, as Sartre indeed thought, these were in some sense unreal, since there is nothing else it could be. And the values must be objective in the straightforward sense that they can be only *objects* of consciousness, they could not be *in* consciousness, they could not be *subjective*, since there is *nothing* in consciousness. Let me emphasize that this conclusion is

intended to follow not from a specific phenomenological examination of moral or ethical consciousness, but from the phenomenological examination of consciousness in general.[38]

Why cannot this rationale be used to support the reality of supervenient properties? Of course, I am talking about a nonreductive supervenience. If all that supervenience happens to be is a reduction to natural properties or is merely a formal definition, then we have our answer as to why Butchvarov's program of defending the reality of moral properties does not apply. But if supervenient properties are experienceable, i.e., given to consciousness, then why cannot it be the case that the form of Butchvarov's argument for the reality of the generic property goodness also holds for supervenience? Why cannot there be a consciousness that is directed to supervenient propertes as well as one directed to ethical properties? Of course, I believe it is conceivable that there is. Another proposal may be offered, however.

Butchvarov may respond, 'Why bother with the notion of supervenience if you find so many parallels between it and my concept of generic properties? Why not simply treat what you call the supervenient property of the self as a generic property? That is, whenever you identify what you call the self, why not simply treat it as being on the level of what I call abstract entities (in the case of goodness, abstract goods such as pleasure, happiness, etc)? John Doe's self is an abstract entity subsumed under the generic property of 'selfhood' or (it would probably be better to generate a neologism since the term 'selfhood' is already used to depict particular combinations of qualities pertaining to personality and/or character) 'selfdom'. Selfdom, then, in the area of identifying or individuating persons would be the analogue of the generic property of goodness in the area of ethical analysis. I am almost persuaded that this could be the case. Since there are strong parallels between what I call nonreductive supervenience and Butchvarov's abstract entities and generic properties, why fight the good fight of nonreductive supervenience against the reductivists, against ontological interpretations of supervenience, etc.?

The question is whether understanding the self as a supervenient quality should give way to understanding the self as an abstract entity analogous to the way Butchvarov understands abstract goods such as happiness, pleasure, life, justice, etc. Certain concrete entities can exemplify these abstract goods. If anybody happens to read this passage, then he/she is exemplifying the abstract good of life. These abstract goods in turn exemplify a property of higher generality, viz., the generic property of goodness. The parallel between the qualities pertaining to the self and those belonging to the moral realm if we were to appropriate Butchvarov's program and use it for our understanding of the nature of the self would seem to be 1) that the physical and psychological qualities of the human individual would be on the same level as that of Butchvarov's concrete entities, 2) that the individual self would be on the level of abstract goods, and 3) that a generic property of 'selfdom' would be on the plane with the generic property of goodness. A further compatibility would seem to exist in the way both the property of the self and abstract goods are given to the consciousness as indicated above.

Ontological economy and the problems associated with supervenience would appear to tip the balance in favor of interpreting the self in terms of Butchvarov's program. It would not serve my purpose very well to call into question Butchvarov's use of the phenomenological interpretation of consciousness's reception of abstract entities because it or something like it would have to be used in respect to showing how an abstraction such as a supervenient quality is delivered to one's awareness.

There is one problem, however, that militates against my using the abstract entity notion for an interpretation of the self, and that is the problem of discerning a strong analogy on the level of the self and abstract entities. If we are allowed the presumption that each human self is unique in its selfhood (the 'Gestalt', the 'pattern', the 'flavor', – choose whatever metaphor you like in order to obtain the notion that each self has its own nonrepeatable character), then each grouping or collocation of physical and psychological properties that comprise a particular human being gives rise to selves that are not identical to one another. This is quite different from the situation of that of abstract goods. It is Butchvarov's contention that the quality of happiness, for example, is a universal and, as such, must be identical from exemplification to exemplification. So, if John Doe is manifesting the abstract good of happiness, then he is manifesting the *very same* abstract good that Mary manifests when she exists in a state of happiness. The requirement that abstract entities operate according to the concept of identity may be the case in respect to the abstract goods of the realm of morality. I am not disputing this point; however, it can be seen that if the notion of the self is analogous to the notion of abstract entities, then it too should be considered a universal quality – identical in each separate instantiation of those clusters of physical and psychological qualities making up different human individuals. But we simply do not treat selves as being identical to one another. The self belonging to Mary is not the same as the self belonging to John (if in fact both have selves because of the complicating requirement that the application of the term 'self' to a human individual may be honorific [an 'achievement' term] as well as 'descriptive').

Now, in *Skepticism in Ethics*, Butchvarov defends the subsumption of the different abstract goods under the generic property good using the concept of identity understood, however, as 'identity in difference'.[39] That is to say (if I understand him correctly), that even though happiness differs from life, and life differs from pleasure, etc., nevertheless, each of these abstract entities are identical in the sense that each exemplifies the higher level generic property of goodness. We cannot (for reasons of length) engage in a summary of Butchvarov's defense of either identity being the basic notion in ontology or his use of it relative to the generic property of goodness at this time. (See Chapter 4 of *Skepticism in Ethics* for both accounts.) It would seem that his approach could apply to the self in the sense that each individual self exemplifies the generic property of 'selfdom' and *in that sense* is identical to other selves even though each self retains its own particular character as, for example, does happiness when compared to life even though both are species subsumed under the generic property of goodness. Now, this sense of identity in application to the self is acceptable because, after all, one has to account for the classification of the self as a self. But this matter of classification does not get at the problem of identity relative to the self I mentioned above. What I was claiming earlier was that if one treats an individual self as being on a level analogous to the abstract goods (entities), then whereas happiness itself functions as a specific universal that can be instantiated by different entities, the self, in turn, cannot function in a similar manner. It itself is not a universal at any level even though it is a property. It is more akin to being a particular that is a property than it is to being a universal. If it is not treated as such, then we will lose the uniqueness that is attributed to human selves.

Does my claim that the self is a property with the characteristic(s) of a particular suggest that Keith Campbell's notion of abstract particulars or tropes provides the proper rationale or support for my understanding of the nature of the self? Not specifically so. Although I concur with both Butchvarov and Campbell that individual things are 'clusters of qualities'[40] or 'compresent bundles of abstract particulars (tropes)',[41] Campbell's analysis of tropes does not capture the notion of the self as I have been using it. (I must interject here that although Butchvarov and Campbell seem to be similar in their understanding of individual things, they differ on the nature of the qualities constituting the individual thing. Butchvarov treats qualities as universals, and identity is the principle by which the recurrence of similarities is explained. In contrast, Campbell treats qualities as particulars [abstract] or tropes, and resemblance is the principle by which recurrence is explained. These differences are profound.) The reason Campbell's trope theory does not work for my concept of the self is that the self would have to be a cluster of tropes – both physical and mental tropes. In this case, the notion of the self would not differ from the notion of the human individual or the human being. The latter too would be the clustering of mental and physical tropes. As Campbell says, 'A human being is a complex of tropes.'[42] Now, it is possible that self and the individual human being in question are absolutely identical, and therefore, 'self' and 'human being' mean the same thing, but the way I have been interpreting the term 'self' is in the sense that a human being may have a self that serves as the (here come the metaphors) 'Gestalt' or 'pattern' or 'character' of those physical and psychological tropes making up the human being. This 'Gestalt' supervenes upon the mental and physical tropes and is simply not identical to them. Simply bundling the tropes together does not get at this concept I am trying to defend. We do become aware of our self, for example, in the case of making difficult decisions. In these cases, we realize that certain options and not others are appropriate to our 'story' or our personal history. Furthermore, we have some inkling of our 'Gestalt' in the way others relate to us, etc. To capture this sense of 'self', and to avoid the problem of the loss of uniqueness of the self that I sensed in Butchvarov's program and the loss of the concept of self in Campbell's theory, I must remain with the concept of supervenience.

At the same time, if Campbell's approach were not so 'anti-supervenience', then I could see my interpretation of the self as a non-reductive supervenient property in terms of its being a trope or abstract particular. Even though Campbell rejects supervenience as a basic ontological category, there is no reason to reject the 'reality' of supervenience as I argued above in respect to Butchvarov's use of a Sartrean view of consciousness in his defense of values as being objective.

Actually, it would appear that Campbell does not object to the possibility of supervenient properties per se. He simply does not want supervenience treated as a basic ontological category. In his book *Abstract Particulars*, he makes this interesting statement:

> Now although the field trope view admits of materialism as a metaphysic, it does not require it. This is a merit of the position. The philosophy of abstract particulars is an ontology, a first philosophy. It should leave open, as far as possible, such plainly *a posteriori* issues as whether the world contains non-physical realities.[43]

It is thus my understanding that Campbell's theory of tropes allows for either a reductive materialism or a dualism in respect to the body-mind problem.

Obviously, I do not want to be classified as either a reductive materialist or a dualist, and it is encouraging to see Campbell take this non-committal stance in the debate because there does not seem to be anything about the theory of tropes or abstract particulars that disallows the possibility of supervenient properties being considered tropes. To claim that supervenience is not a basic metaphysical relation does not take away its being real.

Campbell makes the following helpful statement:

Having set those on one side [some mental tropes may turn out to be derivative physical tropes], the issue becomes whether there are other mental tropes that turn out not to be derivative physical ones. Here the traditional view maintains its appeal: the distinguishing mark of the non-physical mental tropes is involvement with one kind or another of *consciousness.* Sensations (*qualia*), intentionality (understanding) and emotion (a combination of these two) are exactly those mental phenomena that so stoutly resist physical glosses and that incorporate consciousness.[44]

Campbell opens the doorway to his theory allowing supervenient properties when he acknowledges that on the basis of trope theory mental tropes could be non-physical without needing a special "support":

Even if they are non-physical, they do not require a complete new substance to be their bearer. They do not call for a special kind of stuff, with indefinitely many unknown and unsuspected further features, to make non-physical mentality possible. In this way the trope view is more receptive to dualism than most of the ontologies in implicit use in the materialism debate.[45]

In fact, he goes so far as to give some credibility to the supervenience thesis in the very next sentence:

Abstract particularism is certainly compatible with physicalism, but it does relieve some of the pressure towards reductionism, whether of the strict or of the more plausible supervenient kind, which a science oriented substance/property ontology generates.[46]

So, if a trope approach can be used in respect to a non-reductive interpretation of mental events, then it would appear that there is nothing about trope theory that would rule out an interpretation such as mine that the self is a supervenient trope or abstract particular. That is, one can argue that the claims Campbell has made for the possible non-reductive nature of tropes constituting consciousness or mental events can also be extended analogically to the notion of the self. Just as 'sensations (qualia), intentionality (understanding), and emotions (a combination of these two)' can resist reductive interpretation, so can the self as a trope. The self as character, as a pattern of decision-making, as a predictable respondent to an environment (social or natural), or as 'narrative identity' (in the sense that Paul Ricoeur uses the term)[47] is certainly identifiable not only by the individual bearing this self but also from a third-person perspective. The first-person perspective on a particular self may not always correspond exactly with the third-person perspective, but what is interesting here is that at least a third-person perspective is possible, which is not the case in regard to tropes constituting consciousness or mental events per se.

I can make a prediction of how I (the second 'I' referring to my 'self') will behave in a certain situation. So also can a friend of mine make a similar prediction about my behavior in that situation. It is not surprising when the two predictions turn out to be very similar to one another. If a close match does not occur, the agent and his/her friend can give reasons for their respective predictions based on the pattern of behavioral responses each has identified as typical of the agent over the duration of their association with one another. 'Didn't you realize that I cannot stand . . .?' 'Well, yes, but I thought that such and such usually allows you to overcome that distaste for . . .' The agent is not at all insulted by the friend making a prediction; rather, he/she is disturbed that the friend was not accurate in his/her prediction. One's self is not 'private'; it is 'public'.

At this point, it will be helpful to indicate what kind of structure of the self is emerging from the discussion so far. The supervenient self is that which provides the basis for ascribing personal identity to a human being. It should also be noted that the self and consciousness are not identical. If we assume that Sartre had hit upon something phenomenologically correct – i.e., that consciousness itself is not an object but is that which entertains objects of thought and itself is empty of content – then it cannot serve as that which is reidentifiable in time. (Compare this notion of consciousness to G. H. Mead's 'I'.) The self is not to be identified with a person's consciousness. Rather, the self of a person is that abstract outcome of the collocation of physical and psychological tropes peculiar to that individual human being. The self cannot be a *mere* bundle or collection of the individual's properties because, as we will see in Chapter VI, this picture of the self does not do justice to the dynamic role that the self plays in the person's appropriation of time. The self must be both that which provides continuity in time and that which supervenes upon the psychological and physical qualities of the individual. This combination of constituting factors of the self can only be accomplished if the person bearing the self is temporal through and through. The person through its consciousness must be that which identifies its self (that which has supervened upon physical and psychological properties of the past) as the self of the present moment (again, that which supervenes upon the physical and psychological properties *now*) that projects ahead into the future the self that will inform the person given its successful accomplishment of realizing its plans and desires.

Of course, the latter point makes sense only if the person's consciousness and the self can in some fashion be involved in a causal process that leads to the objective conditions as envisioned by the person projecting itself into the future. In the next chapter, I will engage in a discussion of how a materialistic, non-reductive view of consciousness and the self can allow them to have causal efficacy in a physical world. As has been the case, I must argue analogically from the discussion that has emerged in respect to the body-mind problem and see whether a defense of the mind as being a physically dependent, yet distinguishable, entity can serve my claim that the self, as a trope, can have causal efficacy.

**Notes**

1. George F. Stout, 'The Nature of Universals and Propositions', *Classics of Analytical Metaphysics*, ed. Larry Blackman (Lanham, MD: University Press of America, 1984), 176.
2. Ibid., 181-82.
3. Ibid., 186.
4. Ibid., 177.
5. Ibid.
6. Ibid., 177-78.
7. W. V. Quine, *Quiddities* (Cambridge, Mass.: Harvard University Press, 1987), 24-26.
8. Stout, 'The Nature of Universals and Propositions', 179.
9. G. E. Moore, 'Are the Characteristics of Particular Things Universal or Particular' in Blackman, 198.
10. Panayot Butchvarov, *Being Qua Being* (Bloomington, Indiana: Indiana University Press, 1979), 191.
11. Ibid., 194.
12. See the first two chapters of *Being Qua Being*.
13. Ibid., 79.
14. Ibid., 200-201.
15. Donald C. Williams, 'Universals and Existents', *Australasian Journal of Philosophy* 64.1 (March 1986): 6.
16. Ibid., 7-9.
17. Ibid., 8-9.
18. Ibid., 9.
19. Butchvarov, 53.
20. Ibid., 187.
21. Ibid., 78-79.
22. Ibid., 201-202.
23. D. W. Hamlyn, *Metaphysics* (Cambridge: Cambridge University Press, 1984), 100-101.

24 Butchvarov, 147.

25 Some readers may question Butchvarov's distinction between 'nonintentional consciousness of an entity' and 'intentional consciousness' which normally is understood to be 'of' an entity. However, Butchvarov is supported by psychological studies in information processing. See the distinction between 'controlled processing' (focusing on one intentional component at a time) and 'automatic processing' (at the level of the consciousness of entities but not attending to them at a level of awareness) in Richard M. Shiffrin and Walter Schneider's 'Controlled and Automatic Human Information Processing', *Psychological Review* 84 (March 1977): 155-171.

26 Hamlyn, 99.

27 Post, *Metaphysics*, 118.

28 Butchvarov, 165-83.

29 Ibid., 165.

30 Ibid., 165-66.

31 Ibid., 166.

32 Ibid., 168.

33 Panayot Butchvarov, 'Realism in Ethics', *Midwest Studies in Philosophy* 12 (1988): 403.

34 Owen Flanagan, *Consciousness Reconsidered* (Cambridge, Mass.: The MIT Press, 1992), 9-10.

35 Panayot Butchvarov, *Skepticism in Ethics* (Bloomington, Ind.: Indiana University Press, 1989), 53.

36 Keith Campbell, *Abstract Particulars*, (Oxford: Basil Blackwell, 1990) 37. Even so, later in the book Campbell finds the concept of supervenience very helpful in dealing with relations, causality and the social world.

37 Butchvarov, *Skepticism in Ethics*, 56, quoting Sartre's *Being and Nothingness*, p. li.

38 Butchvarov, 57.

39 Ibid., 71.

40 Butchvarov, *Being qua Being*, 181.

41 Campbell, 20-21.

42 Keith Campbell, 'Abstract Particulars and the Philosophy of Mind', *Australasian Journal of Philosophy* 61.2 (June 1983): 131.

43 Campbell, 159.

44 Ibid., 159-160.

45 Ibid., 160.

46 Ibid.

47 See Chapter VII, below.

# 5 Supervenience and action

I have been discussing the relationship between mental phenomena and physical phenomena in respect to what a dependent yet distinctive relationship could be like between the self and its subvening (base) properties. The parallel is not exact, however, in that the self, in our approach, is not identical to the mind. Rather, the mind (and that which would count as constituents of the mind) and the body serve as the subvening properties of the self. Kathleen Lennon's recent book, *Explaining Human Action*, continues the psycho-physical discussion. But her treatment comes closer to my concerns in the sense that she analyzes what the relationship between intentional states and the physical should be in order to allow intentional states to be distinctive from the physical, dependent upon the physical, but nevertheless also *having causal capacity*. I am not sure that it is essential for my purposes that the self have causal capacity. Let us look briefly, however, at Lennon's treatment.

Intentional states pertain to human actions that are not merely reflex in nature nor merely mechanical, but 'the behaviour intentionally performed has some further point or purpose, and in seeking to understand it we also need to know what led the agent to form the intention to act as she did'.[1] Lennon goes on to say,

> When we seek the further point or purpose in our agent's action we are seeking the agent's reasons for intending and acting as she does. Classically an agent has a reason for performing a certain kind of action when she has (a) a 'pro-attitude' towards some end or objective, and (b) a belief that an action of that kind will promote this end.[2]

'Pro-attitude' may be considered to refer to the kind of attitude encompassed by the term 'desire'. Lennon indicates that behavior of the sort that can be typed as intentional can be evaluated as appropriate or inappropriate, and rational or irrational. Both appropriateness and rationality are normative concepts. One can give reasons for intentional behavior, and these reasons are the measure of appropriateness of the act in question. Whether the act is appropriate turns on how the act in question links up with other intentional acts.[3] Even though Lennon acknowledges the normative nature of rationality and appropriateness, she also insists that intentional states have causal capacity. She believes that reasons can *explain* intentional behavior, but she realizes that genuine explanations have normally involved causality. She says, '. . . I shall be giving an exposition and defence of the claim that reason-giving explanations are a sub-species of causal explanations in which the causal links are dependent on the reason-giving ones'.[4]

I will not summarize the arguments that Lennon makes on behalf of intentional explanations involving conditional statements that can be considered as having a causal nature. However, one of her examples that is instructive is the following:

> Imagine that I am driving in Yugoslavia, heading for Dubrovnik, approaching a fork in the road. Given appropriate circumstances the following conditionals will be true of me. (i) If I believe the right fork leads to Dubrovnik I take the right fork. (ii) If I believe the left fork leads to Dubrovnik I take the left fork. These conditionals are true if my choice of route is to be explained by my desire to reach Dubrovnik and my beliefs concerning the road that will take me there. We can express the general form of such conditionals thus: (1) Given C, if R1 then A1.[5]

It would appear that Lennon prefers to think of intentional statements as being of a probabilistic kind because, as she points out, one could desire to sink a certain ball in 'snooker' and yet fail to do so.[6] Nevertheless, she argues for the kind of conditional that would indicate that an intentional state has law-like qualities:

> Again the acceptance of such a conditional claim requires the acceptance of law-like regularities; for if we are to conclude what would be the case in some non-actual situation, we can only do so on the basis of what would occur in all situations of a certain kind.[7]

It is Lennon's belief 'that intentional explanations are causal explanations, and their supporting generalisations empirical causal laws'.[8]

Ultimately, Lennon turns to the consideration of the possibility of a supervenience relation existing between intentional states and physical conditions. It is this kind of relationship that she believes would do justice to the elements she believes are necessary for an *explanation* of the relation that holds between intentional states and intentional acts. These elements are causality, rationality, dependency, and non-reduction.

As far as the laws governing intentional states being reducible to the laws governing physical phenomena are concerned, Lennon uses, as a key point in denying the reducibility of intentional state laws, the principle that 'There must be no explanatory work done by the reduced property which cannot be done by the reducing property'.[9] In order for Lennon to counter Donald Davidson's position that intentional states do not lend themselves to psycho-physical laws,[10] she turns to C. Peacocke's story of Peter's desire to buy a newspaper at a shop that is due to close in five minutes.[11] But if Peter had reason to believe that the shop was already closed, he would have stopped walking in that direction.

> Our understanding of Peter's act requires a grasp of how he would have acted had things been different. It is just by considering what other actions would be appropriate that we work out the conditional implications of our intentional explanations and formulate their supporting generalisations. If the notion of appropriateness is irreducible, so must be the distinctive intelligibility it conveys to the action.[12]

Lennon indicates, further, that 'law-like bi-conditional links [which would be necessary for reduction] between intentional and physical kinds' are not plausible given the possibility that 'Environments which are physically very different can count as evidence, and behaviour physically very different can constitute the same intentional act'.[13] For this reason, Lennon declares that it is plausible to consider 'one-way law-like links between the physical and the mental'.[14] Or, better yet, from her point of view, would be mixed laws which would allow intentional states to have causal power as well as being grounded in physical states. What she is arguing for, once again, is the possibility of law-like conditions obtaining for intentional states without these states simply being considered reducible to physical states. Davidson's position is that such states are non-reducible but upon sacrifice of the possibility of psycho-physical laws. As Lennon points out, Davidson's position in respect to intentional states is to treat them as indeterminate and as having propositional content (that is, they involve propositional attitudes). As such, they fall under normative or rational constraints rather than causal or law-like constraints.[15]

What Lennon wants to do is to deny that intentional states must lose causal efficacy in order to remain subject to normative criteria. At the same time, she does not want intentional states to be reduced to physical states.[16] She wants to remain within the materialist camp. Obviously, in a day that sees a strong movement toward a reductive materialism as expressed by the Churchlands and others, Lennon has a very hard task balancing all of her desires mentioned above. In order to perform this feat, she turns to the concept of supervenience: 'Within current literature non-reductive materialism is characterized in terms of supervenience'.[17]

In order to maintain her materialist position, Lennon ponders the requirement that the subvenient properties (physical properties in the case of the intentional state-body problem) are ontologically prior to the supervenient properties. Lennon indicates that the ontological priority of the subvenient properties is supported by the fact that the subvenient properties can often be found 'in other circumstances and arrangements without any attendant mental properties'.[18] This observation supports the notion that the mental does not give rise to the physical.

Lennon must also maintain that a distinction exists between supervenience and reduction. On the face of it, supervenience seems to have 'nomological links' that move only one way, i.e., from the subvenient properties to the supervenient, whereas '[R]eduction required bi-conditional links, necessary coextensiveness between kinds at each level of description'.[19] This distinction, however, has been called into question by Kim's suggestion that the different groups of subvenient (physical) properties that ground the same kind of intentional properties (supervenient) could be understood in terms of a disjunction. Lennon indicates, then, that

> [i]t would then be the case that there would be biconditional links between intentional and physical kinds, as in cases of reduction. It would simply be that the physical kind was a disjunctive kind. If such a move was accepted it could be extended to the reduction of intentional laws. The physical laws governing the supervenience bases of intentional kinds could be formed into a disjunction and laws at the intentional level derived from them.[20]

Lennon responds to this challenge to the ontological distinction desired by a fair number of the defenders of supervenience by saying that unless the higher-level properties are adequately reduced to the lower-level properties in terms of a unified explanatory theory with no residue of psychological kinds indicated, then supervenience would still be present and not reducible. Of course, it is her contention (as indicated earlier) that unification under an explanatory theory is best served by the rational constraints demanded by intentional action.

However, the question still remains: viz., in what sense is there causal efficacy from the intentional state to the micro level of the physical (neurotransmitters in the brain being activated)? Lennon does not deny that the intentional state must depend upon the physical in order for the intentional act to take place:

> On every particular occasion on which there is a causal connection between an intentional state and intentional act, this connection will be grounded in a physical causal connection between, for example, neuro-physiological states and bodily movements. However, the same kind of intentional causal connection could supervene on distinct physical causal connections on different occasions.[21]

Lennon raises the question that a reductionist might pose; i.e., how can one be sure that the laws governing the intentional state-intentional act level are coordinated with the physical level without resorting to the notion that the former should be reducible to the latter?

This seems to be an unnecessary concern from my point of view. Supervenience, as used by Lennon, is still a dependency relation and not a relation of strong covariance 'in both directions', as favored by Kim. That is to say, the relationship between the intentional level and the physical level is asymmetrical. Even though different physical groupings give rise to one and the same kind of mental event, and even though the mental event in question is distinct from the physical event, the dependency relation guarantees coordination of the two levels of generalization. I believe that the following passage in Lennon states my point in a more formal fashion:

> One move to make in response to this objection is to point out that it is a condition of a physical system realising intentional states at all that its physical states be such that our intentional generalisations come out true. In this sense for every system (or rather for every system in given environments) there is an explanation of how it is, for that system that our intentional generalisations project. This story may however be different for different systems. To ask for a further guarantee as to the projectability of our higher-level generalisations, in terms of vindication by lower-level laws, is to ask for just the kind of reduction which is at issue.[22]

This seems to be a reasonable point on Lennon's part. She is willing to grant the point that a causal relation between an intentional state and an intentional act must be grounded in physical states. That is to say, she is remaining within the materialist's boundaries in that the intentional state-intentional act causal relation is not detached from the physical, and in fact is dependent upon physical cause-effect relationships.

I believe, however, that she needs to engage in a more thorough analysis of the levels of causality and their relationship in order to present a stronger argument against the reductivists. With this concern in mind let us turn to a slightly earlier work by Fred Dretske, viz., *Explaining Human Behavior.* This work is helpful in articulating the relationship that exists between the agent, the intentional state, and the intentional act. In Chapter VI, I will be relying on an existentialist analysis of human behavior and decision making. I believe that Dretske's analysis of human behavior can serve as a 'bridge' between the analytic and existentialist approaches.

Dretske engages in an analysis of the movements of plants and machines and animal behavior in order to shed light on human behavior. He wants us to be aware that for an event to be considered behavior (Dretske considers 'actions' as being synonymous with 'behavior') there must be some 'internal factor' serving a causal role. A train may carry us to Denver, and if our presence on the train was due to 'external' conditions such as our being bound and gagged by fraternity brothers and then being thrown in the luggage car, then that event is not to be considered 'behavior' on one's part. However, if one purchased a ticket to Denver because one desired to go to Denver and boarded the train with the conductor's approval, then that series of events would be considered a form of behavior.[23]

Dretske takes great pains to spell out very carefully the difference between behavior on the part of the organism and mere movements performed by the organism. For Dretske, when authentic behavior takes place, an internal cause is in operation as was indicated above, but the behavior is not merely a product; it is a process. One's trip to Denver, of course, is incomplete until you reach Denver. As Dretske says,

> A process is the bringing about, the causing, the production, of a terminal condition, state, or object – what I have so far called and will continue to call, its product. The product is a *part* of the process, and therefore the process isn't complete until that product is produced.[24]

So, behavior is not merely an emitted event or an 'output'. Dretske sees great danger in treating behavior as output because there is a tendency to

> identify causal explanations of why we *do* the things we do with causal explanations of why our body *moves* the way it does. One will, in other

words, have succeeded in confusing psychological explanations of behavior with neurobiological explanations of motor activity.[25]

He believes that this confusion can be avoided by treating behavior as process instead.

Dretske is quite thorough in his attempt to set the stage for his support of the distinction between causes and reasons and how reasons can still be operable in a world characterized as physical.

He makes it clear that a 'triggering' cause is different from a 'structural' cause. The sounding of a bell may cause a dog to salivate and, thus, be a triggering cause. However, in order to understand why the dog salivated rather than jumped, one must attend to the classical conditioning process that brought about the perceived effect. In this case, the conditioning process is the 'structural' (background conditions) cause(s).[26] The next move that Dretske makes in building a case for human behavior involving reasons as well as neurophysiological states or events is considering how the 'internal' factor plays a role other than that of simply being a physical cause. That is, if one wants to explain why he/she picked up a book and opened it to a specific page, one usually appeals to some *reason* rather than simply being satisfied with a description of the correlation between the firing of certain neurons in the brain and the contracting and movement of muscles and ligaments in the hand that turned the page. The *reason* involves a belief. And beliefs in turn reflect the human's ability to represent 'external' conditions.

Now when Dretske moves to an exposition of how a belief provides a 'map' for the organism to move about in its environment (as does a representational system), there does seem to be a significant difference between his account and that of Lennon in respect to the causal efficacy of beliefs (or intentional states). Whereas Lennon actually attributes to intentional states causal efficacy based on their nomological and explanatory power, Dretske wants to treat belief or meaning in terms of being a characteristic of *that* which has causal power. He illustrates his point with the soprano who has the power to break a glass goblet with her high notes that at the same time have lyrical meaning. Dretske wants us to realize that it is not the lyrical meaning that breaks the glass:

> Trying to exhibit the causal efficacy of meaning itself would be like trying to exhibit the causal efficacy of mankind, justice, or triangularity. No, in exploring the possibility of a causal role for meaning one is exploring the possibility, not of meaning itself being a cause, but of *a thing's having meaning* being a cause or of the *fact that something has meaning* being a causally relevant fact about the thing.[27]

So it would appear that Dretske has given up on reasons as having causal efficacy, but that impression would be precipitous. Dretske engages in an exposition of how indicator systems in plants and animals are able to respond to the environment so that their survival is maintained.

He does not make the mistake of claiming that they have developed response mechanisms in order to find sustenance or avoid a predator. He acknowledges that these capacities are present in the genetic ancestors of these organic entities and they have allowed the organisms to survive in certain circumstances. However, even though these organic entities have representative systems (semantics), these systems are not to be considered beliefs. Representational systems acquire beliefs and not just semantic ability at the organic level where learning is possible. Dretske uses the following symbols in his analysis: C stands for the internal indicator (causing effector mechanisms to operate), F stands for the external conditions detected by the internal indicator, and M stands for the movements that are outcomes of C.

Dretske treats learning in terms of operant conditioning theory. The organism's ability to associate certain rewards with the existence of the conditions of F provides the condition whereby M is realized. Of course, for discrimination learning (a special form of operant learning) to take place, two conditions are necessary, viz., 1) rewards increase 'the probability that the response that generates it (or with which it co-occurs) will occur again in the same circumstances',[28] and 2) the learner needs 'a sensitivity to specific conditions F. Rewards tend to increase the probability that M will be produced *in conditions F*:[29]

> Given these two facts, it follows that when learning of this simple kind occurs, those results (bodily movements or the more remote effects of bodily movements) that are constitutive of the reinforced behavior are gradually brought under the control of internal indicators (C), which indicate *when* stimulus conditions are right (F) for the production of those results. . . . C is recruited as a cause of M *because* of what it indicates about F, the conditions on which the success of M depends. Learning of this sort is away of shaping a structure's causal properties in accordance with its indicator properties. C is, so to speak, *selected* as a cause of M because of what it indicates about F.[30]

So Dretske is asserting that C is a cause of M due to C's indication of what F is. Thus, C has both causal and representational functions. Apparently, then, C attains the status of *belief* in this kind of learning activity.

In this sort of learning activity, C (as representative and as cause of M) serves as the locus of reasons for behavior. Dretske says, 'It is in the learning process that information-carrying elements get a job to do *because* of the information they carry and hence acquire, by means of their *content*, a role in the explanation of behavior'.[31]

A question arises at this point: i.e., To what extent are Dretske's and Lennon's accounts of reasons compatible with one another? Reasons, for Lennon, must be understood in terms of intentional states, and intentional states are supervenient upon physical structures or events. There does not seem to be any difference at this point between Lennon and Dretske in respect to the dependency of intentional states upon physical states. I believe it is safe to say that Dretske's account fits the supervenient approach even though he does not use the term in *Explaining Behavior.*

Dretske's approach allows for what he calls the 'plasticity' of purposeful behavior. The intent here is to show that intentional acts can be realized in a variety of different ways relative to R without R being sacrificed by the variety of possible 'routes' to R. The organism can use different procedures in order to obtain R without the appeal to reasons being vitiated. Reasons do not necessarily explain why a certain procedure is used to obtain R. Rather, they are used in respect to the desired outcome itself:

> Clyde's wanting a beer and thinking there is one left in the refrigerator explains his going to the refrigerator, a process having that particular upshot. They do not explain his taking *that* particular route.[32]

I believe that Dretske has made his case for narrowing down internal indicators to those that can be used for reasons for goal-directed behavior.

A question must be directed to Dretske at this point: The description of reasons, beliefs, and desires relative to goal-directed behavior has been geared to very simple organic systems or goals; however, is this model sufficient to deal with the very complex and long-term future goals of human beings? Dretske is aware of this problem and does indicate that the sharpness of the question can be blunted somewhat by 1) 'response generalization' and 2) observational learning. In respect to the first qualification, Dretske indicates that a rat running a maze in order to obtain food at a certain location can adjust to swimming the maze if in fact it has been flooded. Response generalization may be one way that the complexity of human behavior can be addressed given Dretske's model. The second behavioral adjustment is observational learning. Humans can learn behaviors from watching others even though the learner has never been in an operant conditioning mode relative to the behavior being learned. Observational learning can account for novel behavior. 'Thorndike was wrong. A great deal of what animals learn is observational and imitative learning (see, particularly, Bandura and Walters 1963)'.[33]

Dretske believes that his model does not suffer shipwreck even in respect to the possibility of a human being having a desire for something not yet experienced. One can have a belief that a certain desire leads to R. One also, then, can have a desire for the desire that leads to R. The first desire in this chain is a cognitively mediated desire. Such desires are quite common.[34]

To go along with the possibility of human behavior being based on more involved and complex desires than those affecting other organisms is the necessary concomitant of a more complex set of beliefs and background beliefs. Beliefs in a holistic network can become quite specialized and can change relative to external conditions as well as become associated with other beliefs pertaining to the same external conditions. One can believe that property G is associated with F, and later come to associate H as well with F and, thereby, respond to H relative to F apart from the cognition of G. It is the human's greater capacity to make these associated representations that distinguishes the human from other animal forms. The pigeon can identify a truck represented in a photograph. But, as Dretske points out, can it know as a human child can know that a truck carries things, stops at service stations, stops at rest stops, etc.? The pigeon may be better at picking out trucks than a child; 'nevertheless, this element lacks the cluster of collateral functions, or the network of relations to elements having collateral functions, that helps to define *our* concept of a truck'.[35]

I believe that Dretske's analysis of human behavior is an important step in the direction of an exposition of the nature of the self. I further believe that there is more involved in the constitution of the self than his description of the mechanism of intentional states and acts relative to reasons. But we must not fault Dretske for something he did not intend to do, i.e., give a fuller exposition of the nature of the human self. As Kim points out,

> Dretske does not claim that this simple model, in its present form, is sufficient as an account of the way our beliefs, desires, and other intentional states, with their highly complex and interanimating contents, rationalize our actions. The importance of the model for Dretske lies in that it is a prototype that shows, in a concrete way, the possibility of how a relational representational property of a neural state can causally account for behavior.[36]

Now, Kim's concern about Dretske's account is not the same as mine. My concern is to have a bridge between an analytic, materialistic analysis of human behavior and an existentialist interpretation of behavior that does not seem to be that concerned about the physical-mental relationship existing in the human being. The existentialist seems to be more oriented to the act-side of intentionality as opposed to the intentional state-side. But one cannot neglect either side in an exposition of the human self that might solve the problem of personal identity. It is also necessary to mention, even though in a minimal way, some of the problems encountered in the recent mind-body literature – thus the preceding summaries of Lennon and Dretske's contribution to the philosophy of mind. However, Kim remains a stumbling block. He seems to be impressed by Dretske's attempt to remain a physicalist and still provide an account of mental causality in terms of reasons. But Kim does not think that Dretske has been successful in this attempt. Kim is guided in his analysis of the role that supervenience can play in this controversy (reductivism versus mental causation) by what he calls the 'principle of explanatory exclusion'. This principle is stated as follows: 'there can be at most one *complete* and *independent* explanation of a single explanandum'.[37] Thus, for one and the same act it seems that to have both a neural explanation and a mental explanation (what Kim calls a 'rationalization') is to have causal overdetermination in Kim's eyes. In Kim's estimation, Dretske's attempt to deal with this problem is characterized 'by splitting the explanandum':[38]

> Give each explanation a morsel of its own to chew on and we shall have peace. For Dretske, psychology is in charge of actions and doings, causal-relational structures of the form S(i)-causing-R, and neurobiology and other physical sciences are in charge of events *simpliciter*, such as R.[39]

Kim considers the potentiality of this approach for being dualistic in type. He grants that Dretske is 'a committed naturalist and physicalist',[40] and is, therefore, an anti-dualist. Kim tries to characterize Dretske's attempt to separate the two kinds of explanation as involving relational properties in the case of a psychological explanation of an act and as involving intrinsic physical properties in the case of a neurobiological explanation of an act. Kim indicates that there cannot be a neat distinction between a 'relational explanans and a nonrelational explanans'[41] because R (the results, I presume) varies according to our interest. The R as motor output permits Dretske's kind of approach, but not when R 'involves conditions external to the agent (e.g., the window's being broken, Xanthippe's being widowed)'.[42] I am not sure that Kim is right about this point. Many of the Rs used by Dretske as examples were cases of conditions external to the agent, and it was obvious that intentional states (in the sense of a psychological explanation) were used as reasons for the acts leading to those external conditions. It seems that Kim is aware of his shaky ground here because he uses the typical disclaimer phrase leading into his next criticism. Notice:

*In any case* , even if Dretske is right about the neurobiological being limited in the kind of explanandum it can handle, it still doesn't follow that physical theory, broadly construed, cannot handle these causings as explananda (physics after all is full of relations and relational properties). Unless this is so, nothing follows about a unique or special status of psychology or psychological explanations, and the problem of exclusion remains unresolved. Thus, Dretske's strategy may resolve a potential explanatory conflict between psychology and biology – perhaps for a limited range of behavior involving motor output – but not between psychology and physical theory [my emphasis].[43]

I have difficulty in understanding exactly what Kim demands from Dretske. If one grants that 'rationalizations' as Kim calls them (I will drop the quotation marks from this point on), do in fact exist as explanations for certain kinds of human movement (and Kim seems at least to grant that human beings do in fact rationalize much of their behavior) and one wants to remain a physicalist and not a dualist, then some approach similar to Dretske's seems warranted. Dretske tried desperately to argue the point that internal indicators are physical in constitution yet they can have semantic (representational) meaning. This property of 'aboutness' allows them to be understood from the point of view of intentional systems, and if that is 'psychological' in substance, then so be it. This approach in no way separated the intentional from the neurophysiological, but, of course, one does separate the two in the sense of concentrating one's attention on one of them in the course of discussing its characteristics. Such attention does not imply dualism. In the context of a philosophical discussion, one is, of course, going to focus more attention on the intentional side of things as opposed to the neurophysiological. The latter can be left to the neurophysiologists and experimental cognitive psychologists. One should not be accused of dualism or even moving in the direction of dualism on the basis of one's attempt to describe how reasons can be functional even though the ultimate grounding is the physical.

Kim himself is willing to grant that the appropriate relationship between the physical and the mental is one of supervenience and not of identity.[44] Kim goes on to argue that it is not likely that rationalizations are going to be given up by philosophers relative to the explanation of behavior. What he would like to see happen, however, is an exposition that takes intentions to act as the objects

or explananda, of rationalizations. Another way of putting this is to say that we reconstrue actions as intentions, intentions that we usually think of as *underlying* the actions for which they are intentions.[45]

This switch in attention is supposed to avoid the use of rationalizations as rationalizing physical behavior, and thereby, I assume, ease the problem of mental-physical causation. But, Kim realizes that this approach has its own problems not least of which is: '[w]hat is the nature of the relationship between an intention and the physical behavior that executes it – that is, the relation between my intention to raise my arm and my arm going up?'[46] Kim indicates that this is 'not a rationalizing relation', but he also recognizes that this counter-example does not dispense with the problem of mental causation in respect to physical outcomes.

I do not believe that Kim is entirely fair to Dretske on the issue of rationalizing intentions rather than movements. After all, Dretske did indicate the role that cognitively mediating desires play in complex human behavior, and surely they qualify in some situations as intentions, Thus, rationalizations would have to take into account that type of desire in order to make sense of the movements in question.[47]

One wonders to what extent Kim falls victim to a recent criticism by John Searle of the major actors in the mind-body problem. He claims (among other things) that the Cartesian legacy has left us with a mind-body vocabulary that invariably tends to dualism.

> But notice how the vocabulary makes it difficult, if not impossible, to say what I mean using the traditional terminology. When I say that consciousness is a higher-level physical feature of the brain, the temptation is to hear that as meaning physical-as-opposed-to-mental, as meaning that consciousness should be described *only* in objective behavioral or neurophysiological terms. But what I really mean is consciousness *qua* consciousness, *qua* mental, *qua* subjective, *qua* qualitative is *physical*, and physical *because* mental. All of which shows, I believe, the inadequacy of the traditional vocabulary.[48]

Of course, this is not the only problem Searle has discovered with the mind-body discussion, but I wonder to what extent Kim has fallen victim to it in his criticism of Dretske?

I would like to conclude this chapter with a reference to a rather interesting neuropsychological study performed by Benjamin Libet. This study would support the physical causal nature of making decisions to act, on the one hand, but it would also support a notion of decision-making as a kind of mental causal event, on the other hand. In an article entitled 'Neural Destiny: Does the Brain Have a Will of Its Own?' Libet indicates that subjects were asked to move a hand or a wrist at any time while watching a spot of light revolve on the face of a cathode-ray oscilloscope (something like the sweep-second hand on a clock, but faster) and to report the spot's position the instant they became aware of the decision to act.[49]

What is interesting is that the neuronal activity in the area of the brain pertinent to the decision-making was higher 'a third of a second before they were even conscious of the desire to act'.[50] So, the brain was prepared to act before there was conscious intention to do so. 'Thus, it seemed, even for the most spontaneous decisions, neurological preparation started long before subjects knew their own minds.'[51] Yet, a fascinating follow-up experiment indicated that

> subjects could change their minds during the final one hundred and fifty milliseconds before they flexed their hands and that this moment of possible veto coincided with a drop in the voltage of the readiness potential. Apparently, the conscious mind could intervene, in the final stages of heightened neurological activity, either to block the already initiated movement or to let pass.[52]

This study allows for the feasibility of the contention that a supervenient relationship exists between mental and physical events. What Libet concluded from the study was 'that the brain is continuously generating possible courses of action and that free will operates merely by letting us decide which ones to execute'.[53] Maybe. But the implications for the supervenient relationship are far more interesting.

My primary purpose in summarizing Lennon's and Dretske's analysis of intentional states and acts is to provide grounds for the phenomenological treatment of the self and time presented in the next chapter. As I will attempt to show, the self as a supervenient outcome or property of the person's physical and psychological properties provides the person a basis or context in which decisions are made. And these decisions are based on the person's ability to project him/herself into the future given the person's past and present. Of course this sounds like the standard existentialist or phenomenological approach to temporality, and it is. But the assertion that we are decision-makers needs support, and I believe that Lennon's and Dretske's analyses of intentional states and acts grant a strong measure of plausibility to this assertion. Instead of setting the stage for the next chapter in terms of the traditional problem of freedom of the will versus determinism, I have selected a portion of the contemporary approach to the problem of the causal relation between mental and physical (brain) events because this approach provides another context in which the concept of supervenience can play an explanatory role. The traditional language of the freedom of the will-determinism debate does not usually employ the concept of supervenience.

Further, the Lennon-Dretske material establishes the plausibility of the mental supervening on the physical. In turn, my thrust in this essay has been to suggest that a plausible understanding of the nature of the self is to view the self as a trope supervening on both the mental and the physical. The Lennon-Dretske material thereby serves as an analogy or as a model for my interpretation of the self.

I believe at this point we are ready to consider in the next chapter the roles that time and the community play in the constitution of the self. The role of temporality will be treated from an existentialist or phenomenological point of view, and the impact of society upon the person will be based on G. H. Mead's description of the social self.

**Notes**

[1]  Lennon, 17.
[2]  Ibid.
[3]  Ibid., 34.
[4]  Ibid., 37.
[5]  Ibid., 42-43.
[6]  Ibid., 44.
[7]  Ibid., 44-45.
[8]  Ibid., 45.
[9]  Ibid., 88.
[10]  See 'Mental Events' in Donald Davidson, *Actions and Events* (Oxford: Clarendon Press, 1980), 207-227.
[11]  Lennon, 96-97. Lennon is quoting from C. Peacocke's unpublished manuscript entitled 'Action and the Ascription of Content in Propositional Attitude Psychology', 1979.
[12]  Lennon, 97.
[13]  Ibid., 98.
[14]  Ibid.
[15]  Ibid., 99ff.
[16]  Ibid., 105.
[17]  Ibid., 106.
[18]  Ibid., 112.
[19]  Ibid.
[20]  Ibid., 112-13.
[21]  Ibid., 120-21.

22  Ibid., 121-22.
23  Fred Dretske, *Explaining Behavior* (Cambridge, Mass.: The MIT Press, 1988), 27.
24  Ibid., 35.
25  Ibid., 36.
26  Ibid., 43-44.
27  Ibid., 80.
28  Ibid., 99.
29  Ibid., 101.
30  Ibid.
31  Ibid., 104.
32  Ibid., 132-33.
33  Ibid., 145.
34  Ibid., 146.
35  Ibid., 154.
36  Kim, 'Explanatory Exclusion and the Problem of Mental Causation', 47-48.
37  Ibid., 41.
38  Ibid., 48.
39  Ibid.
40  Ibid., 49.
41  Ibid.
42  Ibid.
43  Ibid.
44  Ibid., 50.
45  Ibid., 51.
46  Ibid., 52.
47  Actually, Kim finds much value in Dretske's account. Kim is so impressed with Dretske's approach that in 'Dretske on How Reasons Explain Behavior' (Chapter 15, of *Supervenience and Mind* [Cambridge: Cambridge University Press, 1993], 285-308), he appropriates the general structure of Dretske's argument and adjusts it by treating the representative content of C (the internal state) as supervenient on a neural state.
48  John Searle, *The Rediscovery of the Mind* (Cambridge, Mass.: The MIT Press, 1992), 15.
49  Benjamin Libet, 'Neural Destiny:  Does the Brain Have a Will of Its Own?' *The Sciences* 29 (March/April 1989): 34.
50  Ibid.
51  Ibid., 35.
52  Ibid.
53  Ibid.

# 6   The self, time, and the community

The difficulties attending the traditional attempts to ground personal identity in either physical continuity (spatio-temporal) continuity or psychological continuity (memory or consciousness) are overwhelming. Derek Parfit's thought experiments appear to be rather conclusive in showing this. Of course, Parfit's interest in the question of personal identity is driven by his ethical concerns. He calls into question ethics that reflects self-interest, and to the extent that the concept of personal identity is presupposed by concern for one's self, that concept is questionable in Parfit's estimation. His approach to ethics is more comfortably situated with a 'no-self' understanding of the moral agent. Thus, a Humean or a Buddhist approach to the self appears to be reflected in Parfit's reductive analysis of the notion of personal identity.[1]

As powerful as Parfit's thought experiments happen to be in calling into question the concept of personal identity, nevertheless, as indicated before, most of us are extremely reluctant to give it up. In spite of very obvious physical and psychological changes occurring in respect to a given individual, we are very much willing to claim that 'That is one and the same person' even if we have not seen that individual for quite some time. We could be given evidence that the individual in question is quite different in a cellular sense; yet, we will maintain the identity of the person in question. Psychologically, also, we could be informed of memory gaps and/or a lack of continuity of consciousness taking place in respect to the human being in question, and normally we would still maintain a belief that this individual is identical to the person we knew long ago.

The usual approach to the problem of personal identity based on a reductive understanding of the human being treats the person as a kind of pseudo-object. That is to say, if the problem of personal identity is to deal with the criterion that pertains to our ability to reidentify a human individual who supposedly persists in time, then the very way of posing the problem seems to use the model by which physical objects are reidentified. This is obviously the model used when a thinker dealing with the problem elects a physical explanation of what a person is. Of course, then, questions of whether the person is constituted by the same matter over a period of time or whether there is at least spatio-temporal continuity in respect to the person's past physical constitution are raised. But even the psychological approach to the problem uses concepts that seem, if not directly based on the physical model, at least indirectly so based. A lack of a memory 'gap' or an 'overlapping' of consciousness (uninterrupted consciousness) provides peace of mind to those who support a psychological interpretation of personal identity. However, one senses behind the use of the terms 'gap', 'overlapping', and 'uninterrupted' the influence of the aspects of a physical model such as spatio-temporal continuity.

Certainly, the simple theory (the theory of soul substance) is based on an understanding of the person as being 'thing-like'. The 'soul', on the surface, seems intelligible in terms of what it does not have in respect to physical properties. Yet one cannot help but notice that the soul seems to have capacities that are causally efficacious relative to the physical world. The interactionist holds that the soul does make a difference in the physical world. Or the dualist can hold that the soul is 'independent' of body, and it is hard to picture this independence and not use physical imagery. Or the soul 'inhabits' a body, and this notion provokes the scene of a homunculus bouncing around in a cranial cavity or something else equally bizarre. With the Lockean criticisms of the concept of the soul, such as that one and the same soul could conceivably occupy a series of bodies, or that more than one soul could logically inhabit a single body, one cannot help it if such thoughts give rise to physical-type images in working through the criticisms. But, the physical model has not really advanced us very far toward a solution to the problem of personal identity.

Using this model simply does not take into account a sufficient number of the relationships existing between the self and time. It is not enough simply to see time as that which flows and occasions questions, therefore, about those aspects of the human individual that permit one to claim that that individual persists in time even though changes occur to that individual that are measured against the flow of time. If the changes are significant and the flow of time is relatively long in duration, then one can wonder if one is identical to his/her self of yesteryear, or one can raise the same question about another individual. Time is not used only in this manner relative to personal identity (that is, as the background against which change is measured). Rather, the very notion of a person and/or self is essentially linked to temporality. As Paul Brockelman says,

> persons are not so much objects over or through time as they are *temporal relations* which shape and form those actions. Selves are not things 'in' time, but temporal *processes* or *dynamic activities.* Selves are tensed. To treat them in terms of 'things' or 'objects' is to fall into a category mistake.[2]

The very notion of a static person is unintelligible.

Suppose that time is real (this is not to imply that it is not real) and independent of human consciousness and, thereby flows without the self being affected by the dynamics of time. In such a case, one would be trying to picture a pristine, underlying self. Such a being is indeed difficult to imagine. I am not saying that it is impossible to develop such a picture, but if one were able to approximate an image such as this, then it would most likely be the choice of some relatively steady state of consciousness such as an underlying (for a short duration at least) sensory quality of color or sound or proprioceptive sensation. Of course, this would not be the grasping of an underlying self, however, because there is more to the self than a relatively short period of uninterrupted consciousness of a sensory quality.

A person is a dynamic unfolding of actions, purposes, realization of purposes, physical qualities and abilities, interactions with other beings and persons, etc. There may very well be an independent reality that can be ascribed to time and its flow, but rarely do we in our existence as persons perceive it in a detached, objective way. What we perceive is our appropriation of time. We appropriate time as we look forward to lunch, plan to eat at a certain cafe, anticipate certain menu items, engage in the physical act of eating, participate in the social intercourse that often accompanies eating that makes it dining, etc. Next we lay aside that particular expectation with its related plans and objectives and *throw* ourselves back into the task at hand. It may be striding down a hallway, opening a door, and greeting a classroom full of students. Even in quiescent moments, such as lying in bed waiting for sleep to come upon us, we do not perceive time flowing independently of the thoughts we entertain – a rundown of the significant events of the day just ended, a resolve not to let *that* happen again, and, possibly, a preview of the expected events of the morrow.

Time does not 'flow' around us. We move in, through, and have our being in time. Having our being is time. It is time that constitutes our very formal nature because our nature is dynamic – 'backward' looking, 'presently' deciding, and 'forward' expecting:

> The unique sense of time we are pointing to here is the fact that human activity is a reaching out of the past and present toward anticipated goals. Action is not 'in' time nearly as much as it embodies the movement of time itself. Putting it another way, we can no more understand an action outside the horizon of the flow and dimensions of time than we can understand breathing without oxygen and lungs. Time – the flow or movement itself – is a necessary condition of our behavior and lives.[3]

As Brockelman's comment indicates, time is a necessary condition of our lives, and action is the human activity that is not only commensurate with the flow of time but that which interprets time for subjects or selves. Brockleman points out (and as we saw in Lennon's account of action) that actions are not merely events, but that action is undertaken in order to produce something or to bring about a goal. And, of course, Lennon emphasizes the 'reason-giving' feature of human actions. Actions, obviously then, are not atemporal. For an action to take place, time is necessary. A person will (in some manner, whether consciously or not) survey the conditions of a situation in order to ascertain whether an act is appropriate, not only in the sense of the probability of an intended outcome, but whether it is even feasible to begin the action in the present circumstances.

As Brockelman and other phenomenologists point out, our actions never take place in a separate, disconnected manner. Rather, they are performed in a horizon of past actions and conditions, continue through a nexus of present conditions and relations, and reach toward a future horizon of goals and anticipated conditions.

As I stride along the hall toward the classroom, I have left behind a discussion with another instructor about a student who has potential but has failed to fulfill it lately. That same discussion has a bearing upon my present condition as I am searching for alternative ways by which to bring the student out of her present morass of indecision and distractedly returning greetings from colleagues and students alike. Having settled upon a tactic relative to the lethargic student, I assume a certain attitude (not necessarily being aware that I have done so) toward that student, and my eyes are directed to her assigned seat as I turn into the classroom at the same time laying plans to call her into my office after class, already having a certain expectation about her response to my suggestions about her academic performance.

Not all of my thoughts and actions as described will, in fact, be in the forefront of my consciousness, that is, in terms of my being specifically aware of them. Of course, if I am entertaining a particular thought, I will at the same time be aware of the activity of thinking, but that is not to say that I turn my consciousness toward the activity and make an 'object' of that activity per se. To do that is to engage in what Sartre calls 'impure reflection'[4] However, the first kind of awareness in which I simply am aware of being engaged in the activity of thinking without making it into an object is called 'pre-reflective consciousness'.[5] A state in between these two types of consciousness is 'pure reflection' which seems to be a deepening of pre-reflective consciousness without it turning the activity of pre-reflective consciousness into an object itself as is the case with impure reflection:

> What Sartre terms "impure reflection" is a form of reflection that is primarily cognitive, giving rise to psychic objects; for example, one can and does make pre-reflective consciousness into an object (of study). Pure reflection, on the other hand, appears to be an apprehension in which the otherness of the pre-reflective remains closely connected to the reflective consciousness, so that the pre-reflective is not posited as an object, as it would be in impure reflection.[6]

It is not my intention to engage in an exposition of the different kinds of consciousness but simply to indicate that different levels of awareness can transpire as a person moves from past to future in his/her daily life.

Our actions are not simply ordered by a succession of discrete 'nows' analogous to beads on a string. Rather, an action is 'lived' through from its inception in the distant or recent past, continuing with renewed dedication in the present and reaching toward an, as yet, somewhat unshaped future. This process of 'living through' an action must be understood holistically:

> Our actions are or contain a sort of *temporal relation* of the past to the future. The anticipation and the conditionality of our actions do not emerge from explicit memory and conscious visualization of the future, as if we existed and acted merely in an atomic and isolated present. That is a common enough misconception of time. Aside from other problems, that would make action meaningless by disintegrating it into discrete fragments which would never add up over time to the interconnected *flow* it actually and necessarily is.[7]

Brockelman, like Heidegger and Sartre, seems to support the notion that lived time gives rise to clock-time:

> But it is not just that actions in general manifest time in the sense of a temporal 'flow'. They also reveal in themselves the 'dimensionality',

'seriality', and 'continuity' of time; and it is through our actions that we become 'aware' of time and 'measure' it with various kinds of clocks.[8]

In contrast, I do not believe it is necessary that clock-time be posited as a derivative of lived time in order for one to emphasize the very nature of one's self as being temporal through and through. I am trying to indicate that an action (an event of human activity manifesting purpose) can only be understood in terms of the unity of the past bearing upon the present and the present taking further shape from its expectation of future realization. The self is to be understood in terms of 'tensed' time without, of course, one dispensing with 'sequential' time.

However, to say our selves and our actions are temporal through and through is not to say that 'real' time or clock-time cannot exist without lived time. As Peter McInerney indicates in his very fine analysis of time in *Time and Experience*,

> . . . Heidegger draws the wrong ontological conclusion from his insightful analysis of now-time (our explicit commonsense conception of what time is like) as a derivative form of world-time. He is quite right that we do not and could not experience simply in terms of now-time. As interested acting consciousnesses, we always encounter other entities in terms of our action-oriented world with its world-time. However, even though now-time must be conceived by a consciousness whose system of meanings is structured in world-time terms, this does not make now-time dependent upon world-time. Only the conception of now-time is dependent upon a lived world-time. It is perfectly possible that a real now-time could exist independently of our conceptualization.[9]

McInerney takes the terms 'world-time' and 'now-time' from Heidegger. 'World-time' is time understood in terms of action, and thus planning, scheduling, expecting, etc., are activities of world-time. 'The most direct way in which world-time has the character of significance is that every moment of world-time is understood with respect to some actual or potential action.'[10] Because world-time deals with the 'significant', it is the source of the 'datability' of events. In contrast to world-time, now-time is the commonsense understanding of time, and it is sequential time – the passing of 'nows'.

> Now-time is ordinarily thought to be a peculiar type of present-at-hand entity that intrinsically passes. Such time is composed of parts or 'nows' that are sequentially ordered and that have a 'privileged part' (the present), which constantly changes in the direction of later dates.[11]

I will treat as at least rough approximations world-time as lived time and now-time as clock-time.

Obviously, now-time may exist independently of lived time even though the latter may help the self gain an awareness of now-time through abstraction. I use the word 'abstraction' inasmuch as the present or 'now' of lived time is so much more filled with meaning and value as opposed to the "now" of now-time in which each case, each now, merely seems to be characterized by identical durations and a specific location in the flow of now-time. In distinction, the 'now' of lived time (world-time) is 'the moment of decision' (to borrow and alter a phrase from a popular contemporary evangelist) and is, therefore, quite different from the sequential nows.

As Brockelman points out, the present or now of lived time is the time of decision, a time of activity that characterizes the present 'now' as being different from other nows. The 'now' of lived time is characterized by and is the site of the continuation of an action generated in the past. The 'now' is the linchpin of an action extending from the past into the future:

> The present is a sort of horizon of activity in which the very sense of being 'present' involves an immediate past and future. What I am doing is the result of what I did before, and it points to what I will do later. It is not so much that I explicitly recall the past or explicitly envisage the future, although I can do that. Rather, I seem to have them in hand and their immediacy bears upon my action 'now'.[12]

Of course, it should be clear that a given sequential now might not serve only as the locus of the lived present in which a given action is continued from the past into the future, but a sequential now can also serve as the locus of a present of lived time in which a decision to generate a new action takes place.

So far what has been said about the human individual being temporal through and through has been very intuitive and non-formal. It is not necessary to be very formal in this exposition in order to see that a problem arises very quickly, viz., if my claim that our reluctance to dismiss personal identity is based on the fact that personal identity cannot be understood correctly without interpreting the person as temporal, then does not this introduction of temporality simply exacerbate the problem of change in respect to the person? If the person is temporal through and through and if the person exists only in the constant movement of past through the present to the future, then in what sense can identity be attributed to this person in process? If anything, it would seem that the introduction of the person as essentially temporal dashes any hope of locating anything about the person that persists or endures in time. Paradoxically, this is not the case.

*What persists in time and is the outcome of the dynamics of the person is the self.* At this point, I must recall that the terms 'person' and 'self', as I use them, are not identical in meaning. I have tried to be careful to use 'human being' or 'human individual' as applying to an individual in a merely designatory manner – as merely picking out some being from other physical beings. (Similarity in physical qualities and/or spatio-temporal continuity would be the minimal attributes denoted by these terms within the context of our discussion of personal identity.) The term 'person' carries more conceptual weight encompassing the attributes of 'human being' (and/or 'human individual') and also the characteristics of temporality demanded by the capacity for purposeful behavior or action. I intend to use the term 'self' to stand for that which is reidentifiable in the dynamics of the person. It is the self that permits us to declare that the person has personal identity.

The self, once again, is a supervenient particular dependent upon the physical and mental characteristics of the person. However, the self is not identical to the person. Rather, it is the 'outcome', the 'picture', the 'pattern', or the 'character' of the person in question, whether it is from the first-person point of view or from the third-person point of view. The sense one has of his/her own character need not be identical to that of another person's impression of him/herself. Not only is this the case, but it is conceivable that the self is not unalterable in the person's dynamical interaction with the world and its contents.

I believe that it is extremely important to be aware of the necessity of distinguishing the self from the person. Other ways of making the distinction are certainly possible, e.g., the 'I' and the 'me' of George Herbert Mead, or the 'consciousness' and the 'ego' of Sartre. (However, I would not claim that my distinction is identical to those of Mead and Sartre.) Without engaging in either an exposition or analysis of how Mead conceives of the genesis of the self, let me simply, at this point, use his notion of the self to support the intelligibility of my own view of the self. As we will see, Mead does not focus primarily on personhood as being constituted by temporality, but his exposition of the self cannot avoid the centrality of temporality in his analysis of the 'I' and the 'me'.

Mead indicates that we can conceive of our own selves because others have taken an attitude toward us:

> This is just what we imply in 'self-consciousness'. We appear as selves in our conduct insofar as we ourselves take the attitude that others take toward us, in these correlative activities. . . . We take the role of . . . the "generalized other". And in doing this we appear as social objects, as selves.[13]

What is important to my purposes here is that Mead provides support to the notion that one can take a perspective upon oneself, and that which is delivered to that gaze is the self. What is not delivered is the person in its full dynamic relationship to time and the consciousness that is involved in that relationship. Society's perspective on oneself is, of course, the third-person point of view. What is interesting in Mead's contribution is that the first-person point of view on the self is prompted by the third-person point of view.

I have not inadvertently moved to a consideration of George Herbert Mead's understanding of the self. Both Ernst Tugendhat and Mitchell Aboulafia are recent thinkers (not to mention Maurice Natanson, who wrote on Mead's philosophy in 1956) who have found Mead helpful in their treatment of the nature of consciousness and selfhood. Maurice Natanson understands Mead to be comparable to a phenomenologist in his work, as opposed to the traditional categorizing of him as a social behaviorist.[14] As Tugendhat points out, Mead engages in a genetic approach to the self whereas both Tugendhat and I are more interested in a 'structural' view of the self. Nevertheless, it does no harm to indicate briefly Mead's view of the genesis of the self inasmuch as it sheds some light on the structural nature of the self.

For Mead, the self originates in a social situation; it does not become aware of itself spontaneously. Nor does it arise apart from society in an isolated, disparate way.[15] Self-consciousness arises in the activity of one individual communicating with another, not in the sense of producing a gesture (that is most likely verbal) that merely elicits a response from the recipient. Rather, the one that is communicating places himself in the position of the other and is able to ascertain the attitude the recipient takes in respect to his/her gesture.[16] A general statement reflecting Mead's point of view in respect to the development of the self is the following:

> The individual experiences himself as such, not directly, but only indirectly, from the particular standpoints of other individual members of the same social group, or from the generalized standpoint of the social group as a whole to which he belongs. For he enters his own experience as a self or individual, not directly or immediately, not by becoming a subject to himself, but only in so far as he first becomes an object to himself just as other individuals are objects to him or in his experience; and he becomes an object to himself only by taking the attitudes of other individuals toward himself within a social environment or context of experience and behavior in which both he and they are involved.[17]

Mead illustrates the ability that the human individual has in appropriating the position through examples of play, in particular role-playing.

Children at an early age play at being teachers, doctors, cowboys, etc., without reflecting upon the role-playing itself, and thus are not *self-conscious*.[18] However, this is a necessary step by which the individual acquires the ability to become conscious of the attitudes others take toward us. The activity of play is without organization or rules, and the roles are played with no awareness of the interdependency of roles, e.g., the cowboy role in reality requires a ranch owner's role.

At a higher level, that of the game, the individual is truly socialized because playing a role at this level demands an awareness of the interdependency of the role played vis a vis others. David Miller points out that one of Mead's favorite examples of games is of baseball. Each player must be able to insert him/herself in the role of the other players in order to do well at one's own position.[19] In being able to entertain the attitudes of the others on the team, one is also able to ascertain the role one is playing in the eyes of the others which can then translate into one's being aware of one's own role.[20] At the level of the game, then, is invoked conscious role-playing, organization, and rules.

In reaching the level of the game, the individual still has not achieved a fully functioning self until it is able to appropriate as its own experience the attitudes of the organized group toward its own activities and processes. When this level is reached, the individual has made contact with the so-called 'generalized other' (a term made famous by Mead). In fact, the individual does not truly think unless it can appropriate the attitude of the generalized other toward itself:

> But only by taking the attitude of the generalized other toward himself, in one or another of these ways, can he think at all; for only thus can thinking – or the internalized conversation of gestures which constitutes thinking – occur. And only through the taking by individuals of the attitude or attitudes of the generalized other toward themselves is the existence of a universe of discourse, as that system of common or social meanings which thinking presupposes at its context, rendered possible.[21]

Not only is thinking determined by the individual's encounter with the generalized other, but so is its conduct. It is the generalized other that provides the norms or standards by which the individual conducts itself.[22] The self is not fully developed until it appropriates the attitudes of the generalized other for its own:

So the self reaches its full development by organizing these individual attitudes of others into the organized social or group attitudes, and by thus becoming an individual reflection of the general systematic pattern of social or group behavior in which it and the others are all involved – a pattern which enters as a whole into the individual's experience in terms of these organized group attitudes which, through the mechanism of his central nervous system, he takes toward himself, just as he takes the individual attitudes of others.[23]

As we will see later, Mead's emphasis upon the self as a social self is confirmed by thinkers such as Tugendhat and Ricoeur. The impact of society on the nature of the self cannot be ignored, as it so often is, when it comes to the problem of personal identity.

The fully developed self has two major aspects, according to Mead, viz., the 'I' and the 'me'. The 'me' aspect is the 'object' aspect, i.e., the 'me' is the self treated as object by the self. This process is, of course, accomplished when the individual is able to appropriate the attitudes of others toward him/herself and is able, then, to be conscious of what it is like to be the object of those attitudes. This process can be accomplished by the individual treating him/herself as an object as have others:

> As a 'me', according to Mead's analysis, the individual is aware of his self, as we have already seen, as an object; he reacts or responds to himself taking the role of the other. It is the taking of the sets of attitudes of others toward one's self that gives one a 'me'.[24]

The 'me' is composed of the attitudes, norms, habits, etc., of the organized group as the self has experienced and appropriated them.

Further, the 'me' is the aspect of the self that conducts itself in terms of what is counted as right as interpreted in its relationship to the generalized other.[25] The 'me' provides, therefore, control over the self, and this control becomes more clear once the nature of the 'I' is spelled out. However, before we turn to the 'I', let us look at a long passage by Natanson in which he refers to the 'me' as having a second and deeper level than the 'me' interpreted as conventional control. In this passage, Natanson is interpreting Mead's understanding of the self in a temporal manner:

> More profound, perhaps, is the notion of the 'me' at a different level at which the 'me' represents a sort of apperceptive mass, i.e., the totality of the content of the past actions and thoughts, the memories of the individual as these are constantly being added to in human experience. What is left out of the 'me' in this sense is the act to be found in the

immediate present: the novel emergent that transcends the 'me'. As, then, a sort of apperceptive mass, that 'me' includes the past, present, and projected future acts and attitudes accomplished, presently available or concluded as being open for accomplishment to the extent that acts in all temporal dimensions are related to a stable and somehow permanent structure of the self. Continuity and transition are qualities of such a structure, for they look back to a content of past deeds that are still part of the self and they look forward to possibilities that are grasped in terms of *my* possibilities, possibilities of a 'me'.[26]

It seems to me that Natanson has imported into Mead's approach to the temporality of the self a rather large amount of existentialistic interpretation. Certainly, Mead would agree that his notion of the 'me' is highly dependent upon the past and 'involves getting memory images'.[27] However, the kind of unified structure an existentialist phenomenologist such as Brockelmann sees in the actions of the person, such as taking up the past and then deciding to act in the present moment upon the basis of the past and the anticipation of the future, does not seem to appear in Mead's analysis of self in *Mind, Self, and Society.*[28]

The reason I believe this to be the case is that Mead understands the 'I' to be quite spontaneous and prone to the novel. He indicates that, of course, we do look to the future as having certain contents based on past and present decisions. He refers to keeping contracts and promises as an example;[29] however, the 'I' is the primary 'actor' in the present moment. And, as such, one can never be sure of what action will finally be undertaken in the present. The 'I' is the response of the individual to the 'me' as a set of organized attitudes provided by the others but assumed by the individual:

> I want to call attention particularly to the fact that this response of the 'I' is something that is more or less uncertain. The attitudes of others which one assumes as affecting his own conduct constitute the me', and that is something that is there, but the response to it is as yet not given.
> . . . Suppose that it is a social situation which he has to straighten out. He sees himself from the point of view of one individual or another in the group. These individuals, related all together, give him a certain self. Well, what is he going to do? He does not know and nobody else knows.[30]

So, the response of the individual to the attitudes assumed by the 'me' has a certain amount of freedom or novelty about it:

The 'I' gives the sense of freedom, of initiative. The situation is there for us to act in a self-conscious fashion. We are aware of ourselves, and of what the situation is, but exactly how we will act never gets into experience until after the action takes place.[31]

Mead indicates that the 'I' is not conscious of itself in an immediate sense as it acts in the present moment.

The 'I' can be aware of its past activities, but as such it has become part of the 'me'. The 'I' cannot be an object to the 'I' – only as it becomes part of the 'me' does it have the characteristics of an object:

> The 'I' of this moment is present in the 'me' of the next moment. There again I cannot turn around quick enough to catch myself. I become a 'me' in so far as I remember what I said. . . . It is because of the 'I' that we say that we are never fully aware of what we are, that we surprise ourselves by our own action.[32]

So, Mead treats the 'I' as the locus of freedom, novelty, and spontaneity in respect to the two aspects of the self.

Mead emphasizes the point that the 'I' and the 'me' are distinct from one another, yet make up one 'personality':

> The 'I' both calls out the 'me' and responds to it. Taken together they constitute a personality as it appears in social experience. The self is essentially a social process going on with these two distinguishable phases. If it did not have these two phases there could not be conscious responsibility, and there would be nothing novel in experience.[33]

The 'I' is the unpredictable partner of the 'I-me' pair; however, Mead acknowledges that the 'I' must conform to the parameters of the 'me'. 'They are separated and yet they belong together'[34] ;nevertheless, Mead refuses to make the 'I' conform totally to the 'me'.

> The 'me' does call for a certain sort of an 'I' in so far as we meet the obligations that are given in conduct itself, but the 'I' is always something different from what the situation itself calls for.[35]

Now, what I understand the self to be is very similar to what Mead calls the 'me'.

Mead's 'I' would simply coalesce with or be a function of the person's consciousness in my estimation. Mead does not seem to want to place any 'content' in the 'I' even though he indicates that it plays a role in the identification of oneself:

> If you ask, then, where directly in your own experience the 'I' comes in, the answer is that it comes in as a historical figure. It is what you were a second ago that is the 'I' of the 'me'. It is another 'me' that has to take that role. You cannot get the immediate response of the 'I' in the process. The 'I' is in a certain sense that with which we do identify ourselves. The getting of it into experience constitutes one of the problems of most of our conscious experience; it is not directly given in experience.[36]

As was indicated above, the 'I' must be compatible with the 'me' if one is going to acknowledge that the "personality" is not fragmented at all times. But it is also clear that Mead is not going to allow the 'I' to be absorbed by the social 'me'. The very nature of the 'I' will not permit such absorption.

Mead maintains the individuality of the personality in two ways. The first is based on individual perspective. Even though the 'me' is the outcome of the appropriated attitudes and role-playing of the individual vis a vis society, the self has 'its own unique pattern'.[37]

> [b]ecause each individual self within that process, while it reflects in its organized structure the behavior pattern of that process as a whole, does so from its own particular and unique standpoint within that process, and thus reflects in its organized structure a different aspect or perspective of this whole social behavior pattern from that which is reflected in the organized structure of any other individual self within that process . . .[38]

However, the individuality of the self is not merely due to the person's unique perspective on its position in the societal nexus. There is the nature of the 'I' itself.

Thus, the second reason for the person's individuality has to do with the ability of the 'I' to respond to the individual's relationship to the society and its attitudes in which it finds itself. The 'I' with indeterminate character is capable of saying 'Yes' or 'No' to society; it is capable of inducing changes in the society at large. Mead cites as examples the changes wrought by the logicians at the end of the 19th and the beginning of the 20th century in respect to the prevailing formal logic of the day. He also points to Einstein as an example of an individual making a fundamental change 'in the form of the world'.[39] These fundamental changes are really the outcomes of almost 'imperceptible' changes due to different persons. These are based, in general, on the fact that

> [t]he individual, as we have seen, is continually reacting back against this society. Every adjustment involves some sort of change in the community to which the individual adjusts himself. And this change, of course, may be very important.[40]

It should be clear that the kind of temporality that the phenomenologist discerns in the structure of the self is very similar to that which Mead understands.

I believe that the difference between Mead's interpretation of temporality and that of the phenomenologist lies in how each interprets the posture of the human individual toward the future. I have the impression that for the existentialistic phenomenologist the individual – whether Dasein or the For-Itself – is able to preview more adequately or has a better grasp of the possibilities provided by the future than does the individual as interpreted by Mead. The 'I' of Mead seems, because of its inherent indeterminacy, to inject a significant amount of indeterminacy into the future.

As I mentioned above, it seems to me that, instead of Mead's 'I' serving as the source of novelty and as the respondent to the 'me's' appropriation of the organized attitudes and activities of society, it would be more economical to combine Mead's 'I' with consciousness itself, i.e., a consciousness similar to Sartre's interpretation thereof, because it is not entirely clear that the 'me-self' as understood by Mead is without awareness on its part.[41] The novelty and freedom that Mead locates in the 'I' is analogous to the ability of the pre-reflective consciousness as described by Sartre to distance itself from the objects of the world and even itself. As noted above, for Mead the 'I' calls out the 'me' and responds to it. However, this action of the 'I-self' vis a vis the 'me-self' could just as well be carried out by consciousness if, as indicated, it is interpreted along Sartrean lines.

Mitchell Aboulafia presents the Sartrean view in brief compass:

> For Sartre, consciousness is the nothing that separates from itself in the act of becoming aware. One cannot be aware of something without at the same time being apart from it, for 'consciousness of anything has to be supported by a negative relation – without which the difference between consciousness and its object would collapse' [Aboulafia quoting H. Dreyfus and P. Hoffman's 'Sartre's Changed Conception of Consciousness: From Lucidity to Opacity']. But note that consciousness is not only in a negative relation to some object outside itself, it is also in a negative relation to itself, just as time is. It cannot be aware of itself

without becoming negative, because it is this negative relation that allows consciousness to be aware – to be aware of objects and to be aware of itself in being aware of objects.[42]

Now, Mead's 'I' is not a totally independent entity vis a vis the 'me'. The 'I' has a tonality consistent with that of the 'me' in spite of its surge of novelty into the future. This point seems to reflect a characteristic on the part of Mead's 'I' that is not available in the Sartrean view of consciousness, and, therefore, it would seem that Mead's position is the more acceptable in spite of its lack of economy.

However, our treatment of Sartre's view of consciousness to this point is based on *The Transcendence of the Ego*. But Aboulafia points out that in *Being and Nothingness* Sartre's view of consciousness is less 'impersonal' inasmuch as he believes that Sartre's treatment of the pre-reflective consciousness there bears a sense of self or selfness. This is not the same as Sartre's Ego that was described in *The Transcendence of the Ego* and retained in *Being and Nothingness*. Sartre's Ego seems to be more akin to Mead's 'me-self'. It is the quasi-object of consciousness. 'The ego is an object of consciousness that is produced as consciousness attempts to thwart its spontaneity through reflection.'[43]

The 'selfness' of pre-reflective consciousness is understood by Sartre to be the movement of consciousness in its sense of lack. That is, selfness refers to the possibilities of the individual and thereby refers to the future of the individual:

> As I move through the world, as I make my daily rounds in the world, a sense of self – of my possibilities, of that which I lack – permeates my pre-reflective consciousness. It is only because there is a plentitude of Being that there can be possibilities, but at the same time, for Sartre, it is only in relation to my possibilities that there is (my) world at all, properly speaking. I am always with myself, even when the self is not actively being produced by reflective consciousness in the form of an object.[44]

Thus, the functions of Mead's 'I-self' can be understood as analogous to the functions of Sartre's pre-reflective consciousness. I believe that this is an important point inasmuch as Mead's description of consciousness is somewhat anemic in contrast to that of Sartre's.

Mead's consciousness has two 'imports'. The first operates on the level of 'awareness' or 'consciousness of', and the second is that of 'appearance of'. The second import has to do with the tendency of the perceiver to place in the 'consciousness' the characteristics of objects perceived at a 'distance' when those objects have constituents (elements) at a micro-level that prohibit the instantiation of the characteristics associated with the object at the macro-level:

> If, then, the reality of things is to be found in these ultimate elements, these other characters must be lodged somewhere else than in the things. They have been placed in consciousness. Consciousness becomes our experience of things not as they are but as they impress us from a distance which we can never overcome except in imagination.[45]

Notice that this understanding of consciousness seems to depict consciousness as a kind of passive receptor of perceptual qualities. Mead denies that perceptual qualities are subjective. He argues that they really belong to the object of perception, but this avowal does nothing to remove the impression that he sees consciousness as a passive perceiver.[46]

The other import of consciousness occurs in respect to the experiences of the self. Mead reiterates a description of his understanding of the genesis of the self. In the process of the individual gesturing to another, the individual positions him/herself in the other's mode of response, then he/she is able to address him/herself as well as address the other. Consciousness occurs when one is able to talk to oneself.[47] In the process of appropriating the other's sense of what a gesture signifies to the other and then what it signifies to oneself, the self emerges and is able to distinguish itself from others and other objects:

> Furthermore, in the process of conduct in which he observes himself acting over against other things and persons, what belongs peculiarly to the agent, who has thus been brought into the field of experience as an object, will be called 'conscious'.[48]

Mead is aware that these two imports of consciousness seem disconnected from one another. He denies that the 'appearance of' import forces sensory or perceptual qualities into 'the mind'. That is to say, whatever is the case about the nature of the object at its micro-level that serves as the basis for the qualities of the object at the macro-level does not mean that the latter are wholly mental when experienced by us: 'In so far, the contact value becomes mental, but this does not render the distance values mental or justify the reference of them to a self as states of consciousness.'[49]

Further, he asserts that because of experimental science as it performs research (and therefore when 'new objects' arise), the 'social human individual' through the use of significant symbols is able to organize possible situations with their objects. These are there as selections and organization of stimuli and symbolized responses only in his own situation and dependent for their achievement upon the situation's maintaining itself in individual and social conduct.[50]

It is debatable to what extent the 'self import' of consciousness is similar to that of Sartre's pre-reflective consciousness. The radical "distancing" of consciousness from itself emphasized by Sartre seems missing in 'the social human individual' as understood by Mead. Although Mead's self seems to be aware of itself as being different from other selves and the objects of the world, it does not blanch at treating itself as being merely another social object.

Mead seems more concerned about having the self with its consciousness fit the social context. Undoubtedly, this concern can be traced back to the influence that John Dewey had upon him during the early days of Mead's career, in the sense that Dewey emphasized at that time that one should try to understand an organ's function in a holistic manner rather than according to a simplistic stimulus-response model.[51] Of course, it was noted above that

> the individual, as we have seen, is continually reacting back against this society. Every adjustment involves some sort of change in the community to which the individual adjusts himself.[52]

But this passage hardly suggests a major rupture between consciousness and its intentional objects as indicated in Sartre's work.

Maurice Natanson asserts that Mead's conception of the self and consciousness does not do justice to the individual's 'inner time consciousness'. For Natanson, neither Mead's 'I-me' distinction within the self nor his interpretation of consciousness provides a coherent description of the ability of the individual to reflect upon the stream of consciousness as it bears upon the 'I' and 'me' aspects of the self:

> [T]he reflecting self is neither identical with the content of the stream of consciousness inspected nor to be confounded with the 'I' and 'me' aspects indicated by that content: the reflecting self (which we may now call the 'ego' for the sake of terminological clarity) is not a 'self' in Mead's terms and has neither 'I' nor 'me' aspects. It is the burden of a theory of inner time consciousness to study the relationships pertaining between the ego and the stream of consciousness, but this can be done only by exploring the ego as a transcendental ground of consciousness.[53]

Thus, for Natanson 'Mead's theory of the self, then, lacks foundational articulation.'[54]

Natanson goes so far as to claim that 'Mead presents a theory of the self that lacks a conception of consciousness.'[55] However, this statement seems to be based on Mead's statement that 'consciousness as such refers to both the organism and its environment and cannot be located simply in either'.[56] Natanson, then, claims further that the description of consciousness in the *Philosophy of the Act* does nothing to soften his criticism. However, this claim by Natanson refers to a statement about consciousness in the section entitled 'Miscellaneous Fragments' in which Mead describes consciousness as 'inner conversation and is in the field of symbols'.[57] But Natanson ignores Mead's analysis of the import of consciousness bearing upon the self that I outlined above. Surely, the 'self-import' of consciousness is not merely a reflection of consciousness as a relationship between 'the organism and its environment', nor merely an 'inner conversation'.

The 'self-import' analysis allows for self-consciousness – at least in the sense of how the individual can be aware of his/her distinction from others and physical objects and of his/her social context and what his /her individual position happens to be within that context. Certainly, this passage from Chapter IV of the *Philosophy of Act* should negate the notion that Mead's view of consciousness did not allow for a sense of 'inner time consciousness' even though he did not develop the theme to maturity:

> Finally, the inner conversation of significant symbols, which we call 'thought', and the flow of imagery in reverie, the one involving the self in its double capacity and the other attaching to the self as its past history, constitute a central core of what is called consciousness.[58]

It may be the case that Mead's view of consciousness does not have the reflective power that is found in Sartre's view, but on the other hand, neither does Sartre's view have the constructive view of the input of the social dimension upon the self that Mead's does.

Undoubtedly, as Aboulafia clearly points out for the Sartre of *Being and Nothingness*, the other is extremely important, if not necessary, for the individual to be fully conscious of being a person. The other's look treats one as an object, and one experiences this objectifying of oneself by the other. However, this experience of oneself being objectified is rejected by one's consciousness just as one's consciousness never can totally accomplish the objectification of itself. One's consciousness refuses to be totally objectified whether it is attempted by another subject or by oneself:

The me-as-object, my being-for-others, is my 'outside', my 'nature'. I recognize and accept it as my outside. I am a subject that can and must become an object for other(s), for if I did not have the me-as-object as an outside, I would have no way of differentiating from the other (pp.286-287). However, I do not have to remain solely this me. Because of the freedom of (my) consciousness to not be what it is, I can escape from the me which I am for the other and myself. My consciousness is then not reduced to the me but negates it, distances itself from it.[59]

But, as Aboulafia points out, the dependency of the person upon the other for a full awareness of oneself as subject comes about through confrontation with the other. Each person tries to objectify the other. 'Hence, there is a war of each against the other, each trying to maintain his subjectivity against the Medusa look of the other.'[60]

Thus, society of a sort (at least in *Being and Nothingness*) is necessary for the development of subjectivity within the Sartrean program, but it certainly does not resemble the organized, cooperative relationship existing between the individual and society as described by Mead. If one could combine (and I see no reason why it would be inconsistent to do so) the negating, distancing power of consciousness as described by Sartre (which provides the individual with the ability to make evaluations and discriminating judgments) with the constructive, organizing character of the appropriation by the individual of the goals, values, and attitudes of society as described by Mead, one would be on the way to a more apt description of the nature of consciousness and self-consciousness.

In the next chapter, I will attempt to show that the self, as it is constituted by time and the community, can be understood as a 'narrative identity' that cannot be identified apart from the values inscribed by the community and used by the person bearing the self.

## Notes

[1] Parfit, 502-03. See James Duerlinger's corroboration of Parfit's belief that his 'no-self' theory is similar to that of certain Buddhist schools of thought in 'Reductionist and Nonreductionist Theories of Persons in Indian Buddhist Philosophy', *Journal of Indian Philosophy* 21.1 (March 1993): 79-101.

[2] Paul Brockelman, *Time and Self: Phenonenological Explorations* (New York: The Crossroad Publishing Co., 1985), 12.

[3] Ibid., 22.

4   Mitchell Aboulafia, *The Mediating Self: Mead, Sartre, and Self-Determination* (New Haven: Yale University Press, 1986), 33.

5   Ibid., 32.

6   Ibid., 32-33.

7   Brockelman, 24.

8   Ibid.

9   Peter McInerny, *Time and Experience* (Philadelphia: Temple University Press, 1991), 145-146.

10  Ibid., 123.

11  Ibid., 125.

12  Brockelman, 29.

13  Aboulafia, 11, quoting Mead's 'The Genesis of the Self and Social Control', in *Selected Writings*, 284.

14  Maurice Natanson, *The Social Dynamics of George H. Mead* (Washington, D.C.: Public Affairs Press, 1956), 145-146.

15  George H. Mead, *Mind, Self, and Society* (Chicago: University of Chicago Press, 1934), 140.

16  Ibid., 140-141.

17  Ibid., 138.

18  David L. Miller, *George H. Mead: Self, Language, and the World* (Austin, Texas: University of Texas Press, 1973), 51.

19  Ibid., 52.

20  Mead, *Mind, Self, and Society*, f.n. 7, 154.

21  Ibid., 156.

22  Ibid., 154-55.

23  Ibid., 158.

24  Natanson, 15.

25  Ibid.

26  Ibid., 15-16.

27  Mead, *Mind, Self, and Society*, 176.

28  Ibid., 177-178.

29  Ibid., 203.

30  Ibid., 176.

31  Ibid., 177-78.

32  Ibid., 174.

33  Ibid., 178.

34  Ibid.

35  Ibid.

36  Ibid., 174-75.

37  Ibid. 201.

38  Ibid.

39  Ibid., 202.

40   Ibid.
41   Gary A. Cook, *George Herbert Mead: The Making of a Social Pragmatist* (Chicago: University of Illinois Press, 1993), 64.
42   Aboulafia, 30.
43   Ibid., 35.
44   Ibid., 37.
45   George H. Mead, *The Philosophy of the Act*, ed. Charles W. Morris, (Chicago: U. of Chicago Press, 1938), 74.
46   Ibid., 74-76.
47   Ibid., 75.
48   Ibid.
49   Ibid., 76.
50   Ibid., 78.
51   Cook, 72.
52   Mead, *Mind, Self, and Society*, 202.
53   Natanson, 61.
54   Ibid.
55   Ibid., 62.
56   Mead, *Mind, Self, and Society*, 332.
57   Mead, *Philosophy of Act*, 659.
58   Ibid., 75.
59   Aboulafia, 40-41.
60   Ibid., 40.

# 7 The self and narrative identity

Ernst Tugendhat is generally in agreement with Mead's interpretation of the self as being integrated with society. He is particularly commendatory in his analysis of Mead's approach to the individual's appropriation of the rules (norms) of society. Tugendhat notices a similarity existing between Aristotle's understanding of community (koinonia) and Mead's 'generalized other' or 'organized community or social group'.[1] For both Aristotle and Mead, cooperation among its members is the foundation for the concept of community, and it is rules (norms) that allow a community to be constituted:

> Furthermore, it is only in the case of norms governing cooperative practices that it seems self-evident that for every obligation of one individual there are corresponding rights of other individuals. . . . Mead speaks of the 'generalized other' not just because attitudes of the 'social group' are at issue but also because these attitudes are normative expectations; and this implies that they are generalized demands. These expectations do not simply arise from all the individuals of the group, but they are grounded in the organization of cooperation within the society. They are directed toward the individual, not as an individual, but as the bearer of specific roles . . . .[2]

At this point, Tugendhat indicates that the self has its sense of self-understanding through the role it plays within the social nexus:

> In adopting a role I understand *myself* as a so-and-so; and since I develop a definite character in the multiplicity of roles, the issue in a more significant sense becomes who (what kind of a person) I want to

be, that is, how I understand *myself*. What is contained in this 'myself' or 'oneself'?[3]

In respect to this question 'What is contained in this myself?' Tugendhat claims that Mead does not address it adequately. Mead's concept of 'talking to oneself', Tugendhat seems to hold, is tied to the role-playing of the second level of the emergence of the self (Mead's game level) instead of the first level (play level). For Tugendhat, this is an inadequate attempt to describe the self's self-understanding because one can play a role without identifying with it. Playing a role may not be self-fulfilling in itself.[4]

In spite of this difficulty, Tugendhat sees more merit in Mead's approach to the self through society than is available in Martin Heidegger's approach. Mead provides the rudiments, at least, of the self finding meaning in its existence through the affirmation of others as they appraise the role elected by the individual in question:

> Now if Mead had talked to Heidegger, he would have advanced the following thesis: (a) we only find meaning in a form of life that we can regard as worthy of esteem along with others; and in connection with this, (b) the relevant activities are those that we engage in not only for ourselves but at the same time for and with others: that is, cooperative activities. . . . [T]here is nothing in Heidegger that corresponds to the first part of the thesis – namely, to the idea that the will can only fulfill itself in something that is 'good' in the sense that it requires intersubjective recognition.[5]

At this point, Tugendhat engages in an attempt to provide a defense of how the 'good' can be ascertained, but I do not want to engage in that discussion. Suffice it to say within this context of concern that relative to an individual and his/her self-understanding, a striving for excellence in some abilities is an attempt at advancing the good – especially if the abilities are judged excellent within an intersubjective setting.

Tugendhat raises the pertinent question: Why is this 'striving for excellence in some abilities' relevant to the relation of one's self to oneself?[6] Tugendhat discusses three levels in respect to an answer to this question. However, I will simply collapse them into the idea that when abilities are exercised in relation to a role and when they are exercised well relative to the agent's 'social place' that has 'a long-term cooperative function', then the agent will have developed 'a relation to *himself* and a feeling of self-worth'.[7] This sense of worth relative to one's role is not sufficient, however, according to Tugendhat, because one can always advance the further question 'What kind of person do I want to be?' as opposed to the more elementary 'answers such as "a good teacher", "a good mother" . . .'[8] This latter point, though, is only hinted at by Mead and not developed by him.

This inadequacy on the part of Mead's description of the self and its self-consciousness is exacerbated, according to Tugendhat, by Mead's focus on roles at the expense of the 'affective'. What kind of person I want to be involves more than effective role-playing, viz., the human qualities – such things, I suspect, as friendliness, loyalty, veracity, etc. For Tugendhat, the affective is even more basic than role-playing because the affective can have a bearing, first, upon the choice of a role for oneself and, second, on how the role is exercised according to the human qualities and not just in terms of how efficient the agent is at playing the role.

Even if Mead did not develop this particular point, Tugendhat finds Mead more advanced than Heidegger on the topic of the relationship obtaining between the self and society. Tugendhat indicates that Mead's 'I', even when it acts in the mode of 'self-assertion' and calls into question the conventions and norms of society, still acts with society as an impetus or motivation for his/her act. Tugendhat quotes Mead:

> A man has to keep his self-respect, and it may be that he has to fly in the face of the whole community in preserving his self-respect. But he does it from the point of view of what he considers a higher and better society than that which exists.[9]

In contrast, when one turns away from the interests of the 'they' of Heidegger in order to achieve authenticity, to what does one turn? It is not a turning to a better 'they'. It is a turning away:

> While the 'they' in Heidegger has no positive significance aside from constituting the actual structure of our everyday existence, the 'me' for Mead has the positive connotation that normative conceptions must first be existent in conventional form in order for a society as well as a relation of oneself to oneself to be constituted. Furthermore, conventionally pre-existent norms provide the only material on whose basis an autonomous self-relation can be worked out; and the result of this work can only be improved conventional conceptions.[10]

The social and moral emphasis brought to bear upon the structure of the self, self-consciousness, and self-determination (self-assertion in Mead) by Tugendhat brings us to the most recent work of Paul Ricoeur.

Ricoeur, in *Oneself as Another*, analyzes the nature of the self relative to personal identity, and he is convinced, as am I, that personal identity, as attributed to the human individual, must take into account the essential role played by temporality in respect to the structure of the self. As does Tugendhat, Ricoeur also understands the necessity of taking the social and the moral into consideration in one's attempt to understand the nature of the self.

Ricoeur begins his work with a linguistic exposition of selfhood in terms of what it means to say that a person remains the same throughout a period of time. He wants to claim that personal identity is better understood as *ipse*-identity rather than *idem*-identity:

> Identity in the sense of *idem* unfolds an entire hierarchy of significations, which we shall explicate in the fifth and sixth studies. In this hierarchy, permanence in time constitutes the highest order, to which will be opposed that which differs, in the sense of changing or variable. Our thesis throughout will be that identity in the sense of *ipse* implies no assertion concerning some unchanging core of the personality. And this will be true, even when selfhood adds its own peculiar modalities of identity, as will be seen in the analysis of promising.[11]

*Idem*-identity corresponds well to numerical identity. There may be some similarity between *ipse*-identity and qualitative identity, but there is not a strict equivalence because *ipse*-identity can pertain to that which not only has similar qualities over a period of time but to that whose being is 'consistent' over time as alluded to in the last sentence of the preceding quotation.

*Ipse*-identity pertains to the person as the 'who' of living and acting as opposed to an *idem*-identity that would pertain primarily to a person as a 'what'. I think it is fairly safe to state that Ricoeur understands the Parfitian approach to personal identity as being based on an *idem*-identity or a 'what' approach. Ricoeur certainly respects the analytic tradition and is interested in the conceptual challenges raised by this tradition, but he believes that the analytic approach fails to do full justice to the problem of personal identity. In order to engage in a 'hermeneutics' of the self, Ricoeur indicates that engaging the analytic tradition in a dialogue about personal identity will be a useful detour:

> In fact, analytic philosophy will direct the wide detour by means of the questions 'what?' and 'why?', although it will be unable to follow all the way to the end the return route leading back to the question 'who?' – *who* is the agent of action?[12]

In passing, let me say that we must not assume that Ricoeur is returning to a Cartesian-ego position:

The overview just presented of the studies that form this work gives an idea of the gap that separates the hermeneutics of the self from the philosophies of the cogito. To say *self* is not to say *I*. The *I* is posited – or is deposed. The *self* is implied reflectively in the operations, the analysis of which precedes the return toward this self.[13]

This passage indicates that Ricoeur belongs on the side of Mead and Sartre in respect to the nature of the self as opposed to that of Natanson and Husserl. The self for Ricoeur is not a transcendental ego.

In setting the stage for his interpretation of personal identity as requiring the concept of *ipse*-identity, Ricoeur refers to Strawson's *Individuals* as a dialogical partner belonging to the analytical tradition. It is not to our purposes here to recount Ricoeur's analysis of Strawson's 'identifying reference'; however, his use of Strawson's notion of 'basic particular' bears comment. Ricoeur indicates that for Strawson the first basic particulars are bodies. (A basic particular is 'a primitive concept, to the extent that there is no way to go beyond it, without presupposing it in the argument that would claim to derive it from something else.')[14] Ricoeur has no difficulty accepting the notion that 'body' is a basic particular, but he is also impressed with Strawson's treatment of 'person' as a basic particular as well. Ricoeur believes that Strawson's treatment of body as a basic particular has merit to the extent that it precludes the possibility that mental events are also candidates for the role of basic particular. If the latter should be the case, then the problem of a mind-body dualism looms before us. However, the disadvantage with treating all predicates, including the mental, as belonging to the body, is the obscuring of the self as a 'who'. For Ricoeur, Strawson's analysis, by and large, follows the route of *idem*-identity, a 'what' approach, and once this is in place, it is extremely difficult to retrieve the selfhood of the person once it is covered over by the emphasis upon the physical.

Ricoeur agrees that neither a mind-body dualism is desirable, nor should we discount the role of the body in its spatio-temporal relations as contributing to the criteria of the re-identification of an individual. But to the extent that the body serves as a paradigm for the concept of a basic particular, the full reality of selfhood will be submerged in the physical:

> . . . [I]n a problematic of identifying reference, the sameness of one's body conceals its selfhood. And this will be the case as long as the characteristics related to possessive pronouns and adjectives ('my', 'mine') have not been connected to the explicit problematic of the self.[15]

Now, Ricoeur agrees with Strawson's notion that the person is a primitive alongside the body. He argues that the notion of a person can be treated as a 'logical subject' to which predicates can be ascribed. However, two kinds of predicate can be so ascribed, viz., 'physical predicates which the person shares with bodies, and mental predicates which distinguish it from bodies'.[16]

What becomes problematic for Ricoeur in giving primacy to the body as one of the possible logical subjects of predication is the use of

> first-person possessive adjectives: *this body as mine.* After all, is the possession implied by the adjective 'mine' of the same nature as the possession of a predicate by a logical subject? There is, to be sure, a semantic continuity between *own, owner,* and *ownership* (or *possession*), but it is relevant only if we confine ourselves to the neutrality of *one's own.* And even under this condition of the neutralization of the self, the possession of the body by someone or by each one poses the enigma of an untransferable property, which contradicts the common notion of property. This is indeed a strange attribution, that of a body which can never be made or taken away.[17]

The same concern can be directed to the ownership of psychic predicates. That is to say, Ricoeur agrees that '"the *same* sense" [can be] ascribed to psychic predicates, whether they are ascribed to oneself or to someone else'.[18] This kind of 'sameness' is also problematic for giving the self its full due. Ricoeur acknowledges that the 'same sense' being applied to psychic predicates enables us to generate the notion of the mind in the sense that we can reidentify psychic predicates whether ascribed to oneself or others, and this suggests that

> there is no self alone at the start; the ascription to others is just as primitive as the ascription to oneself. I cannot speak meaningfully of my thoughts unless I am able at the same time to ascribe them potentially to someone else . . . .[19]

(This 'linguistic' approach seems analogous to Mead's 'experiential' description of the genesis of one's self-consciousness.)

Yet, for all of the affirmative characteristics of the 'sameness' of sense ascribed to psychic predicates, Ricoeur cannot help but repeat the question of whether the expression '"my experiences" is equivalent to the expression "someone's experiences"'.[20] Furthermore, 'ascribing a state of consciousness to oneself is *felt*; ascribing it to someone else is *observed*'.[21]

Although Ricoeur presents some interesting material in its own right in Chapters II-IV of *Oneself as Another,* I do not believe it advances my main concern of ascertaining the nature or structure of the self vis-a-vis its relationship to time. Allow me, therefore, to simply allude to the contents of these three chapters. In Chapter II, entitled 'Utterance and the Speaking Subject', it is clear that Ricoeur wants to make a case for treating the indexical or 'shifter' 'I' as being not merely a term of indication or reference that can be used by any number of speakers but also as having the function of 'fixing' who is speaking. In this latter case, the 'fixing' or 'anchoring' reflected by the utterance of the term 'I' generates an 'aporia' (confusion) because, on the one hand, the anchoring expressed by the 'I' suggests that the 'privileged point of perspective on the world which each speaking subject is, is the limit of the world and not one of its contents',[22] and on the other hand, that the person to whom the 'I' refers *is* part of the world:

> The lack of coincidence between the 'I' as the world-limit and the proper name that designates a real person, whose existence is confirmed by public records, reveals the ultimate aporia of the speaking subject.[23]

Ricoeur attempts to resolve this problem by describing an analogy existing between the 'I' and the deictic 'now' that has two temporal interpretations – 'the living present of the phenomenological experience of time and the indifferent instant of cosmological experience'.[24] The lived-time 'now' is 'inscribed' upon the instant of cosmological time (a model of which is calendar time). 'The dated now is the complete sense of the deictic 'now'':[25]

> The conjunction between the subject as the world-limit and the person as the object of identifying reference rests on a process of the same nature as inscription, illustrated by calendar dating and geographic localization.[26]

The 'inscribing' of the 'I' literally does take place often enough, e.g., on birth certificates (records) of a community:

> From this registration, there results the one who states, 'I, so and so, born on . . . at. . . .' In this way, 'I' and 'P.R.' mean the same person. It is therefore not arbitrary that the person (object of identifying reference) and the subject (author of the utterance) have the same meaning; an inscription of a special kind, performed by a special act of utterance – naming – performs this conjunction.[27]

What is important to our concerns in this linguistic study by Ricoeur is the uniqueness of the self intimated by the speaker's use of 'I' in an anchoring way. The self, as belonging to that which has a 'privileged point of perspective on the world'[28] takes on, to that extent, an individuating mark different from that of any other self in the universe.

In Chapters III and IV, Ricoeur considers the role of the self as agent. In Chapter III, 'An Agentless Semantics of Action', Ricoeur indicates that both G. E. M. Anscombe and Donald Davidson treat action along the lines of a 'what' rather than as a 'who'. In order to counter this oversight on the part of Anscombe and Davidson, Ricoeur in Chapter IV, 'From Action to the Agent', takes Aristotle and Kant out of retirement in order to reintroduce the 'who' into the process of action. I do not think Ricoeur's analysis of Aristotle and Kant really speaks to the problem of the causal relationship (if any) obtaining between the physical body (brain) and the intentional act. He merely, in the case of Aristotle, indicates that Aristotle can be interpreted as holding that the self is the principle of action, and the act of deliberation prior to an action points to the 'who' rather than to the 'what':

> The canonical definition of preferential choice admirably expresses this subtle attribution of the action to the agent through the predeliberated: 'The object of choice being one of the things in our own power which is desired after deliberation, choice will be deliberate desire of things in our own power; for when we have decided as a result of deliberation, we desire in accordance with our deliberation.'[29]

Let us turn to Ricoeur's analysis of Kant and causality relative to the agent.

As I indicated above, Ricoeur's reliance upon Kant's understanding of causality relative to agents does not really address the neurophysiological-intentional relations that are of concern to philosophers today.

In Ricoeur's case, he focuses his discussion on Kant's analysis of causality in respect to human freedom ('Third Conflict of the Transcendental Ideas' of *The Critique of Pure Reason*). The upshot of the discussion is that there is an antithesis between 'causality in accordance with the laws of nature' and the 'causality of freedom'.[30] Kant's solution to the problem points to two kinds of 'beginning' relative to a causal series. The first has to do with an absolute beginning, 'one which would be the beginning of the world'. The second 'is a beginning in the midst of the world'. It is the second type that 'is the beginning related to freedom'.[31]

As Ricoeur points out, it becomes very difficult to ascertain the relative beginning of an agent's action because very different interpretations relative to the action can be maintained.[32] (Compare Anscombe's 'poisoning the political chiefs' example.) On the other end, how far does one extend the ascription of responsibility to the agent in respect to the effects which can be quite extensive in their range? Ricoeur deals with this problem by decision rather than by description: 'We must not be afraid to say that determining the end point where the responsibility of an agent ends is a matter of decision and not some fact to be established.'[33] For all of this, Ricoeur still has not addressed the problem that must be addressed in the contemporary period. He adverts to Kant's treatment of the causality of freedom that has a 'transcendental' cause with effects in the realm of appearance.[34] The effect that occurs in the realm of appearance is called 'character'. Ricoeur believes that Kant is insightful here and extends the position by calling the ability of the agent to alter effects in the world 'initiative'.

Ricoeur is willing, then, in respect to the action of the agent, to allow for different kinds of causality to operate with each other:

> If, at the present stage of our investigation, we can represent this grasp of the human agent on things, within the course of the world, as Kant himself says, only as a conjunction between several sorts of causality, this must be frankly recognized as a constraint belonging to the structure of action as initiative.[35]

I am afraid that this kind of exposition simply allows 'mystery' to enter the topic of causality all too easily. The 'transcendental' causality of freedom making a difference in the phenomenal realm (realm of appearances) kind of approach simply does not address the problem of psycho-physical causality with sufficient sensitivity to contemporary concerns. Not all 'truth' is to be found in the texts of authors of long ago even if one grants the hermeneutical approach some measure of efficacy.

However, having questioned the hermeneutical method, let us look at a very helpful contribution coming from Ricoeur, viz., his exposition of narrative in respect to the nature of the self. Even though Ricoeur's work, *Oneself as Another*, is described as being primarily concerned with the problem of personal identity, I think it is more accurate to describe it as a treatise on the self, including, of course, a concern for the problem of personal identity. Ultimately, the thrust of the book is directed toward the self in relationship to other selves.

Where Ricoeur is most pertinent to our topic is in Chapter V, 'Personal Identity and Narrative Identity'. where he treats the problem of personal identity squarely. This chapter indicates the importance of treating human existence from a temporal point of view if any progress is to be made in respect to the problem of personal identity. Ricoeur sees the self as temporal through and through so that if an identity is to be discovered for the self, then 'in many narratives the self seeks its identity on the scale of an entire life . . . '.[36] Now, this statement was presented in the context of a comment about brief actions to which Chapters III and IV were devoted, in contrast to the 'connectedness of life' stressed by Dilthey. Ricoeur indicates within this context that a proper theory of action needs treatment from a narrative point of view and not simply from the 'bare bones' analytic approach – although Ricoeur makes it very clear that he respects the analytic tradition's exposition of action. Ricoeur further indicates that the treatment of action in Chapters III and IV suffered from not taking temporality into consideration.

In the course of Ricoeur's hermeneutical study of action in Chapters III and IV, it would have been helpful if he had pointed out the problems that face Anscombe, Davidson, Aristotle, and Kant concerning the dimension of time. Merely as a suggestion, when the terms 'motivation' or 'deliberation' were brought into play along with the 'why' (the teleological aspect of action), it would have been salutary for Ricoeur to have shown that action is not merely an event to be treated substantively (as a 'what') as he so deplored in the case of Davidson. Rather, an action not only spans a duration of time but is, in fact, constituted by tensed time. An action, even though picked out of a series of causes and effects, has a past, present, and future. The moment of deliberation must take into consideration the circumstances provided by the past, the deliberation as it proceeds and culminates in a decision in a particular present, and the casting forward with anticipation into the future as to the possible outcomes of the action if put into play.

Ricoeur does make the following statement, in which he deplores

> the priority given to 'the intention-with-which' in relation to 'the intention-to' [which he says] has allowed the attenuation, without ever eliminating it entirely, of the temporal dimension of anticipation which accompanies the agent's projecting himself ahead of himself.[37]

My complaint against Ricoeur is not that he does not notice the problem that comes from excluding temporality from the analysis of action, but that he does not take advantage of the opportunity in which to give, at least, a brief synopsis of how action is temporal through and through – something along the lines I suggested in the preceding paragraph.

Let us turn to Ricoeur's treatment of the self in terms of narrative identity which is obviously highly dependent upon the temporal structure of the self as it engages in action. Ricoeur sets the stage in Chapter V by indicating the typical problem with identifying something as *being the same* over a period of time. He describes numerical and qualitative identity treating them as the criteria of reidentification, and he also refers to uninterrupted continuity as a third criterion. Having treated the concept of identity in terms of 'sameness,' Ricoeur makes this summarizing statement in respect to the problem of personal identity: 'The entire problematic of personal identity will revolve around this search for a relational invariant, giving it the strong signification of permanence in time.'.[38]

Ricoeur immediately offers the very kind of answer that I have been supporting in this analysis of self, viz., the 'relational invariant' is *character*. He also offers a second invariant, viz., *keeping one's word*; however, it seems to me that the latter can be subsumed under the former even though what makes the second model interesting is its obvious dependency upon temporality. The self reveals itself in time as either being dependable or not.

In this chapter (v), Ricoeur returns to the distinction of *idem*- and *ipse*-identity with, of course, the concept of personal identity having more to do with ipse-identity than with idem-identity even though the latter is that which provides the sense of 'invariant'.[39] In this work, Ricoeur sees the need to alter an interpretation of character that he supported in earlier works. That is, 'character' for him had meant 'immutability' in respect to a person's characteristics. In contrast, 'Character, I would say today, designates the set of lasting dispositions by which a person is recognized'.[40] This characterization of character fits very well with my approach to the self as supervenient. In respect to the supervenient self, both the agent and the other is able to discern a 'pattern' or 'shape' in a life-style that identifies the person in question. A pattern or shape that individuates a life-style is the 'invariant' mentioned above by Ricoeur. Allow me to extend Ricoeur's insight at this point.

'Character,', 'pattern', 'shape', or 'narrative identity' are hardly given to the agent or observer in some kind of instantaneous manner. To 'recognize' either one's own character or another's is to have had exposure to the personal history of the person in question. Who we are can only be revealed over time. No momentary flashes of experience will reveal ourselves either to us or to others. All that can be given in an instant is the phenomenal qualities of the body of the self – not the self in itself.[41]

Ricoeur, at this point, tries to weave the 'idem' and 'ipse' self together in the sense that character, even though it evolves, nevertheless, through its characteristics of 'habit' and 'acquired identifications,' has the quality of perdurance – sameness over time. Character evolves in respect to habit in the sense that a habit must, at one time, have been established:

> [h]abit gives a history to character, but this is a history in which sedimentation tends to cover over the innovation which preceded it, even to the point of abolishing the latter.[42]

And, in respect to acquired identifications, Ricoeur is referring to the 'values, norms, ideals, models, and heroes *in* which the person or the community recognizes itself. Recognizing oneself *in* contributes to recognizing oneself *by*'.[43] It is in respect to the assigned identifications that the *idem* and *ipse* identities coincide. '. . . one cannot think the *idem* of the person through without considering the *ipse,* even when one entirely covers over the other'.[44]

The evaluative nature of the acquired identifications provides a rationale for observations such as 'Tim is not himself today' or 'Lily is acting totally out of character lately. It isn't like her to shortchange the waiter'. Thus, character in the sense of both habit and acquired identifications provides the agent and the other with a sense of the self as perduring.[45] Ricoeur sees the concept of character outlined as lending itself to narrative treatment:

> It will be the task of a reflection on narrative identity to balance, on one side, the immutable traits which this identity owes to the anchoring of the history of a life in a character and, on the other, those traits which tend to separate the identity of the self from the sameness of character.[46]

As I mentioned earlier, Ricoeur has a second model besides that of character by which to characterize the essential temporality of the self, viz., keeping one's word.

Ricoeur believes that the 'self-constancy' exhibited in the keeping of promises is a 'polar opposite' to that of the permanence in time reflected by the first model, character. Apparently, it is due to its moral implications that self-constancy is different from character's relation to time. Ricoeur uses in respect to self-constancy the sentence 'I will hold firm' (in regard to keeping a promise) even if my opinions change, my desires change, etc.[47] Ricoeur claims that self-constancy is solely within the dimension of the 'who' as opposed to the more general nature of character. With this distinction, Ricoeur is willing to allow the model of self-constancy to break with *idem-*identity:

> This ethical justification, considered as such, develops its own temporal implications, namely a modality of permanence in time capable of standing as the polar opposite to the permanence of character. It is here, precisely, that selfhood and sameness cease to coincide.[48]

Obscurely, then, Ricoeur claims that the 'notion of narrative identity' that is tied to temporality can somehow mediate between the two models of self-constancy and sameness of character:

> [W]e will not be surprised to see narrative identity oscillate between two limits: a lower limit, where permanence in time expresses the confusion of *idem* and *ipse,* and an upper limit, where the *ipse* poses the question of identity without the aid and support of the *idem.*[49]

But, why should self-constancy be at such odds with character? I fail to see why promise-keeping and, therefore, self-constancy cannot be brought under the aegis of the sameness of character in respect to its 'acquired identifications' aspect. The notion of acquired identifications is certainly normative in its implications. Is it not possible to conceive of promise-keeping as an acquired identification – one of the values of a given community by which one can identify oneself? It seems strange that Ricoeur would want to disengage the *idem*-identity and *ipse*-identity in respect to the character and self-constancy models.

The notion of permanence in time is more easily understood through *idem*-identity – sameness in time. To the extent that *idem*-identity type qualities can also be discovered in human existence, then it is more intelligible to accept the self as character that is the bearer of personal identity. Ricoeur already has admitted that the model of character allows for narrative interpretation; character can be both innovative and sedimented – in the generation of a habit and in the continuation of a habit. There is a great similarity in Ricoeur's notions of habit and of acquired identifications to that of Mead's 'I-self' and the 'me-self' in which both conformity and innovation are to be found. Character, then, allows for narrative description (as Ricoeur already indicated), and the latter does not need to serve in some obscure manner as a mediator between character and self-constancy. Self-constancy can simply be absorbed by character and really be more in tune with an emphasis upon temporality serving as a necessary ingredient in the constitution of personal identity. In fact, Ricoeur's way of describing self-constancy in terms of promise-keeping reverts to an *idem* type of identity in time and makes time an enemy rather than a constituent of the self:

> In this respect [Heidegger distinguishing 'the permanence of substance from *self*-subsistence'] keeping one's promise, as was mentioned above, does indeed appear to stand as a challenge to time, a denial of change: even if my desire were to change, even if I were to change my opinion or my inclination, 'I will hold firm'.[50]

But, such holding firm should not be seen as antithetical to time because what is holding firm is the person *whose* character is such that promise-keeping can only be intelligible in terms of the unfolding of time. The key term 'promise-keeping' does not point merely to a quickly moving event. Rather, to signify anything intelligible, the term points to a speech-act made in the past, a decision in some present or 'now' to fulfill the promise, and subsequently the performing of an act that was in the future relative to the decision to keep the promise.

Promise-keeping is a process that does not challenge time; rather, it works through time in order to be what it is. Of course, there is a constancy between promise declared and promise fulfilled in the sense that the speech-act of promising refers or alludes to an act still in the future by which the speech-act is discharged. But this is not a constancy that 'challenges' time as if time itself were the source of threat in terms of change to the person carrying out those announced intentions such as promises. Time has no ability to change anything. Rather, it falls to the conditions of things that 'materialize' within time to have the power to make a difference to other conditions also existing in time.

The agent, in conformity with his/her character that has developed in terms of habit and acquired identifications, discharges the duty laid upon him/herself by the speech-act of promising. The constitution of personal identity, then, in such a case is not that of some static thing-like entity that suffers no change whatsoever in the process of keeping a promise. Instead, what is 'constant,' what is 'permanent,' is that expectation by the agent and/or other (who is aware of or privy to the fact that a promise had been made) based on some kind of awareness of the nature of the character of the agent as to the likelihood of the duty being discharged. The person or agent perdures if expectations are fulfilled. Questions about the agent's identity are raised even if only fleetingly if the expectations are thwarted.

In a sense, Ricoeur captures some of my concern in his attempt to show the relationship between the narrative identity of the self and the action contained in the plot of a play or fictional work. Rather than my describing in detail his interpretation of narrative theory which is interesting in its own right, let me simply indicate that he comes to the conclusion that the development of a character in a literary work and the action of the plot are intimately and necessarily intertwined. A literary example upon which he depends heavily is Robert Musil's *The Man without Qualities*. This work is described as a 'fiction of the loss of identity.' It is a narrative, apparently, of a person losing his identifiable qualities. As this story-line progresses, the work becomes less and less a narrative and more and more an essay:

> To see more clearly the philosophical issues in this eclipse of the identity of the character, it is important to note that, as the narrative approaches the point of annihilation of the character, the novel also loses its own properly narrative qualities, even when these are interpreted as above in the most flexible and most dialectical manner possible. To the loss of the identity of the character thus corresponds the loss of the configuration of the narrative and, in particular, a crisis of the closure of the narrative.[51]

In Ricoeur's treatment of the relationship between character and plot, character is 'the one who performs the action in the narrative'.[52] And, just as there is concordance (the principle of order in the story line) and discordance ('the reversals of fortune that make the plot an ordered transformation from an initial situation to a terminal situation'[53]) in the 'emplotment' of action, so is there a dialectic of concordance and discordance in the character:

> The dialectic consists in the fact that, following the line of concordance, the character draws his or her singularity from the unity of a life considered a temporal unity which is itself singular and distinguished from all others. Following the line of discordance, this temporal totality is threatened by the disruptive effect of the unforeseeable events that punctuate it (encounters, accidents, etc.). Because of the concordant-discordant synthesis, the contingency of event contributes to the necessity, retroactive so to speak, of the history of a life, to which is equated the identity of the character.[54]

The point Ricoeur wants to make with this description of character is directed against Parfit. Ricoeur wants to claim that a person 'is not an entity distinct from his or her "experiences"'.[55]

Ricoeur's basic complaint against Parfit's reductionist approach is that Parfit's use of technological fictions (as opposed to Ricoeur's use of literary fictions) to characterize the essential qualities of personhood simply treats the brain as the equivalent of the person.[56] And, then, Parfit applies technological mutations to the brain in order to call into question those approaches to personhood that allow for personal identity. In contrast, Ricoeur believes that his narrative approach respects the person's corporeal nature as it functions within the physical world as a mediator between the self and the world:

> Characters in plays and novels are humans like us who think, speak, act, and suffer as we do. Insofar as the body as one's own is a dimension of oneself, the imaginative variations *around* the corporeal condition are variations on the self and its selfhood. Furthermore, in virtue of the mediating function of the body as one's own in the structure of being in the world, the feature of selfhood belonging to corporeality is extended to that of the world as it is inhabited corporeally.[57]

This point is reminiscent of Merleau-Ponty's interpretation of the body's 'motility,' a kind of intentionality of the body toward the life-world.

Ricoeur believes that Parfit loses this 'existential invariant' which is 'our corporeal condition experienced as the existential mediation between the self and the world'[58] as he focuses on hypothetical technological variations performed on the brains of persons. Ricoeur indicates, though, that deciding between literary fictions and technological fictions might not be possible on the level of the imaginary. It may only be decided on the level of the ethical at which point the actions of the person are not simply analyzed on the level of cause-effect relations but on that of the evaluative and the accountable. In fact, Ricoeur goes so far as to suggest that the very technological manipulations used in a hypothetical way by Parfit, if materialized, would be more than an infraction of present morality and legality:

> Is not what is violated by the imaginary manipulations of the brain something more than a rule, more than a law; is it not the existential condition of the possibility for rules or laws as such, that is, finally, for precepts addressed to persons as acting and suffering: In other words, is not what is inviolable  the difference between the self and the same [in the sense of *idem*-identity], even on the plane of corporeality.[59]

Ricoeur in making this charge, however, has no intention of depriving  Parfit and others of 'dreaming,' of engaging in hypothetical considerations, but he simply hopes that these thought experiments remain simply that.

I want to return, now, to my earlier criticism.  I found nothing in Ricoeur's analysis of character in terms of narrative theory that suggests that character is not enough in terms of its dialectic between *idem*-identity and *ipse*-identity to serve as the basis for self.  There was nothing in narrative theory per se that forces one to include the notion of self-constancy or *ipse*-identity in its 'challenge to time'.  Character, once again, contains both *idem*-identity and *ipse*-identity, and there is no need to assume that one needs a pristine *ipse*-identity to bring the ethical to bear upon the nature of self, personhood, and, therefore, personal identity.

At this point in his treatment of selfhood and identity, it seems to me that Ricoeur has suffered a kind of failure of nerve.  What seems to trouble him is his earlier emphasis upon the person's *ownership* of physical and mental attributes.  It was the ownership theme that set his notion of *ipse*-identity over and against the reductive *idem*-identity approach of Parfit.  It also seemed as if his emphasis upon narrative identity also emphasized *ipse*-identity over and against Parfit's technological variations on the brain.

However, a curious thing happens in Ricoeur's *Oneself as Another*.  Once he takes up a consideration of the concept raised by A. MacIntyre, viz., 'the narrative unity of life', Ricoeur seems to cave in on the notion of narrative identity.  He capitulates in the sense that he sees a problem that he claims MacIntyre does not see, viz., the problem in moving from fictional narrative to the narrative of a life. 'For MacIntyre, the difficulties tied to the idea of a refiguration of life by fiction do not arise'.[60] Now, prior to this point Ricoeur distinguished three levels of meaning that can be discovered in the actions of a life. Practice, the first, has to do with long action chains that can be found in the 'professions, the arts, and games'.[61] and also has 'nested' relations as well. For example, farming as a profession contains 'subordinate actions, such as plowing, planting, harvesting, and so in descending order . . . '.[62] The second level of meaningful action is called 'life plans' by Ricoeur. 'We shall term 'life plans' those vast practical units that make up professional life, family life, leisure time, and so forth'.[63] The third level is MacIntyre's 'the narrative unity of life' in which the first two levels are unified through commitment to ideals and a life project:

> In this sense, what MacIntyre calls 'the narrative unity of a life' not only results from the summing up of practices in a globalizing form but is governed equally by a life project, however uncertain and mobile it may be, and by fragmentary practices, which have their own unity, life plans constituting the intermediary zone of exchange between the undetermined character of guiding ideals and the determinate nature of practices.[64]

So Ricoeur now recounts the difficulties in this understanding of narrative theory being applied to real life in response to the question of 'how do the thought experiments occasioned by fiction . . . contribute to self-examination in real life?'[65] He then raises the following questions: 1) In my life 'story', am I the author or the narrator or the character or all of the preceding three combined? 2) Beginnings in fiction are clear; however, they are not so in real life. Furthermore, in real life, 'endings' are not neat and pat; there can be several endings. Thus, what happens to the notion of a unified life? 3) 'Can one then still speak of the narrative unity of life'[66] if one's life history is in tension with any others' – friends, parents, colleagues? And 4) In our self-understanding, anticipation of and projects relative to the future play a large role. If one's life story is open-ended in this fashion, how comparable is it to fictional narrative?

Now, what is curious is that Ricoeur answers every one of these objections in favor of how fictional narratives can speak to these alleged problems. (We need not recount the answers.) However, later he writes as if the objections are still standing and so much so that these problems, along with a reference to the 'loss of identity' fiction, cause him to take the position that narrative identity offers no advantage over Parfit's assertion that 'personal identity is not what matters':[67]

Self-apophasis consists in the fact that the passage from 'Who am I?' to 'What am I?' has lost all pertinence. Now the 'what' of the 'who', as we said above, is character – that is, the set of acquired dispositions and sedimented identifications-with. The absolute impossibility of recognizing a person by his or her lasting manner of thinking, feeling, acting, and so on is perhaps not demonstrable in practice, but it is at least thinkable in principle. What is practicable lies perhaps in acknowledging that all the attempts at identification, which form the substance of those narratives of interpretive value with respect to the retreat of the self, are doomed to failure.[68]

All of a sudden, in three pages (166-168), Ricoeur has vitiated his entire program. Why? It must hinge on his desire to see the self as primarily ethical (and at this point he agrees with Parfit's rejection of self-interest) instead of in terms of 'ownership'. And, to do this he demands that the 'other' comes to the fore. The narrative self has been 'stripped bare' – 'a fact that should make it clear to us that the issue here is the ethical primacy of the other than the self over the self'.[69]

But, what does a fictional loss of identity have to do with personal identity in real life?

It is a very strange move, indeed, that causes Ricoeur, blinded to his own good insights, to converge upon Parfit's reductive approach to personal identity. That move is simply his taking too seriously the *possible* loss of identity as depicted in Musil's *Man without Qualities*. Here Ricoeur's hermeneutical approach takes a wrong direction. He should have retained his roots, viz., phenomenology. A phenomenological approach would have permitted him to 'see' that narrative identity, in terms of character, is an apt metaphor for what we discover every day, viz., our own self and that of others, and our own character and that of others. We do 'sense' the dynamics of actions performed by persons that, together with certain physical',a 'Gestalt,' a 'character', or 'self', that can be identified time and again.

In Chapters VII through IX (Ricoeur calls these chapters 'studies'), Ricoeur takes up his ethical and moral concerns that are primarily directed by teleological and deontological theories along with excursions into Rawls, Hegel, and Habermas. I see no reason to give a precis of this material as it has little or no bearing upon the problem of self and personal identity; although, at the end of the Ninth Chapter, Ricoeur tries to recapture the theme that initiated his book, namely, the role of selfhood in respect to personal identity. This attempt is reflected in a few paragraphs in which he ties responsibility to temporality. This analysis is very unenlightening. The future of a self in terms of responsibility simply implies that someone assumes the consequences of her action, that is, holds certain events to come as delegates of herself, despite the fact that they have not been expressly foreseen and intended. These events are her work, in spite of herself.[70]

The past comes in for comment as well. Again, Ricoeur's understanding of responsibility commits the person to assuming certain aspects of the past even though it is not 'entirely our own work'.[71]

Both the past and the future

> overlap in responsibility in the *present*. But this present is not the instant as a break, the point-instant of chronological time. It has the thickness that the dialectic of selfhood and sameness gives it, in connection with permanence in time. Holding one-self responsible is, in a manner that remains to be specified, accepting to be held to be the same today as the one who acted yesterday and who will act tomorrow.[72]

Ricoeur does indicate that the sameness of character does have a bearing on 'the recognition of moral identity, in particular in the cases of responsibility that concern civil law and penal law'.[73] But, then, once again he calls upon the

> puzzling cases of narrative identity, where identification in terms of the usual corporeal or psychological criteria becomes doubtful, to the point at which one says the defendant in criminal law is no longer recognizable.[74]

At this point, Ricoeur repairs once again to self-constancy or *ipse*-identity.

In this move, Ricoeur has the subject (a moral subject) in terms of self-constancy accept in the *present* the responsibility for both past deeds and future effects of the person who presently has a *tenuous hold* on narrative identity. Ricoeur recognizes that *ipse*-identity in this case is 'irreducible to any empirical persistence'.[75] He uses the image of the 'great book of accounts' in which the acts of a person are inscribed and therefore, are imputed to that person:

> Perhaps this metaphor of inscription and registration expresses the objectification of what we just called the recapitulation in the present of the responsibility for consequences and of the responsibility for indebtedness. Self-constancy, objectified in this way, in the image of an interlinking of all of our acts outside of us, has the appearance of a fate that makes the Self its own enemy.[76]

But this notion of *ipse*-identity or self-constancy being the dominant metaphor for selfhood seems to vitiate the notion of selfhood as understood by Ricoeur in the preceding quotation!

What is problematic about this move is the following:

1) Temporality as constitutive of the self, and so insightfully ascertained and stated by Ricoeur earlier in this work, is lost in *ipse*-identity in spite of his assertion that

> this responsibility in the present assumes that the responsibility of the consequences to come and that of a past with respect to which the self recognizes its debt are integrated in this nonpointlike present and in a sense recapitulated in it.[77]

*Ipse*-identity is still only operating in the decision of the present and, in principle, is not in continuity with the *idem*-identity of its character because it is *assuming* responsibility for something *it* did not necessarily perform in the past nor is accountable for in terms of effects in the future.[78] So, there really is no personal identity afforded by *ipse*-identity. 2) Even if *ipse*-identity afforded means by which the reidentification of a person were possible, it would do so only for 'moral subjects' – those persons who had enough heroic 'selflessness' to assume the responsibility for those acts attributed to their narrative identity or their character that is now not so ascertainable due to the 'loss of identity' as described in those fictional cases taken so seriously by Ricoeur. What about those recalcitrant types who refuse to take responsibility for their behavior – those who are 'immoral' subjects? Do they have self-constancy or *ipse*-identity? Apparently not, given the way Ricoeur describes self-constancy. 3) *Ipse*-identity seems to be more of an irruption into the narrative 'flow' of the person (as indicated in problem #1 above), and this condition is exacerbated by the lack of the 'anchoring' of self-constancy in the attitudes and mores of society that we saw with the 'I's' relation to the 'me' in Mead's treatment of the self. Even though Ricoeur works through the social features of Aristotle's teleological ethics, the 'universalization' and 'respect for others' of Kant's morality, and the *Sittlichkeit* of Hegel, I still get the sense of a limited impact of the values of the community being appropriated by the self in Ricoeur's treatment as opposed to that of Mead's.

Once again, this would not be the case if Ricoeur did not take the infrequent and exotic cases of the 'loss of identity' fiction as a paradigm for interpreting narrative identity or character (which he admitted is not merely composed of *idem*-identity but of *ipse*-identity as well). Because he makes this move, character treated in the sense of the 'me' characteristics described by Mead (*idem*-identity in Ricoeur's case) is lost, and thus so are the aspects of the 'I' characteristics that are treated by Mead as *belonging* to the self in the sense that the 'I' must have familiarity or commensurability with the 'me' characteristics. Again, if Ricoeur treats the odd case as being paradigmatic for the concept of selfhood, and if *ipse*-identity or self-constancy is a surd relative to the person bearing a character and has no real continuity with character, then why should there be any *reason* for *ipse*-identity to be accountable for or to take responsibility for the person in his/her role of narrative identity or character?

As I see it, the way Ricoeur ultimately interprets *ipse*-identity provides little or no content to the concept of selfhood even though it was to *ipse*-identity that he turned in order to distinguish his program from Parfit's. His best insight into selfhood was the notion of character that, at the outset, contained the dynamics of both *idem*-identity and *ipse*-identity. However, due to the influence of the 'loss of identity' genre, Ricoeur treats character as *idem*-identity and identifies *ipse*-identity with self-constancy and moral decision-making, thereby incurring the negative results I have mentioned above.

Even though Ricoeur does not complete his own good insight into narrative identity or character understood as containing both *idem*-identity and *ipse*-identity, I can certainly claim that his insight, along with Mead's social interpretation of the self, supports my understanding of the nature of the self.

This chapter began with a phenomenological approach to the person's 'lived time.' It was then necessary to show what there was about the person that still allowed for the possibility of personal identity – perdurance in time – even though the tenseness of lived time is dynamical through and through. What persists through the dynamics of lived time is the self – in the case of Mead the combination of the 'I-self' and the 'me-self' and in the case of Ricoeur the narrative identity best understood as character in both its *ipse* and *idem* identities. A problem remains, however, and it has to do with getting clear about the self's relationship to consciousness. We will turn to a treatment of this problem in the next chapter.

## Notes

[1]   Ernst Tugendhat, *Self-Consciousness and Self-Determination* (Cambridge, Mass.: The MIT Press, 1986), 239.
[2]   Ibid., 241-242.
[3]   Ibid., 242.
[4]   Ibid., 243.
[5]   Ibid., 245-46.
[6]   Ibid., 248.
[7]   Ibid.
[8]   Ibid.

[9]   Tugendhat, 253, quoting Mead's *MSS*, 389.
[10]  Ibid., 252-53.
[11]  Paul Ricoeur, *Oneself as Another* (Chicago: The University of Chicago Press, 1992, 2.
[12]  Ibid., 17.
[13]  Ibid., 18.
[14]  Ibid., 31.
[15]  Ibid., 33.
[16]  Ibid., 36.
[17]  Ibid., 37.
[18]  Ibid.
[19]  Ibid., 38.
[20]  Ibid.
[21]  Ibid.
[22]  Ibid., 51.
[23]  Ibid.
[24]  Ibid., 53.
[25]  Ibid.
[26]  Ibid.
[27]  Ibid., 54.
[28]  Ibid., 51.
[29]  Ricoeur, 93, quoting Aristotle's *The Nichomachean Ethics* 3.5 1113a, 9-11.
[30]  Ricoeur, 102.
[31]  Ibid., 105.
[32]  Ricoeur, 71, based on G. E. M. Anscombe's *Intention* (London: Basil Blackwell, 1979).
[33]  Ibid., 107.
[34]  Ibid., 109.
[35]  Ibid.
[36]  Ibid., 115.
[37]  Ibid., 85.
[38]  Ibid., 118.
[39]  Ibid., 121.
[40]  Ibid.
[41]  Of course, it takes some time for a self to develop. However, the recognition of the self by the subject or another can take place rather quickly. See the first section of my concluding chapter.
[42]  Ibid.
[43]  Ibid.
[44]  Ibid.

[45] Ibid., 122.
[46] Ibid., 123.
[47] Ibid., 124.
[48] Ibid.
[49] Ibid.
[50] Ibid.
[51] Ibid., 149.
[52] Ibid., 143.
[53] Ibid., 141.
[54] Ibid., 147.
[55] Ibid.
[56] Ricoeur may be somewhat harsh in respect to this point.
[57] Ibid., 150.
[58] Ibid.
[59] Ibid., 151.
[60] Ibid., 159.
[61] Ibid., 153.
[62] Ibid., 154.
[63] Ibid., 157.
[64] Ibid., 158.
[65] Ibid., 159.
[66] Ibid., 161.
[67] Ibid., 167.
[68] Ibid.
[69] Ibid., 168.
[70] Ibid., 294.
[71] Ibid., 295.
[72] Ibid.
[73] Ibid.
[74] Ibid.
[75] Ibid.
[76] Ibid., 296.
[77] Ibid., 295.
[78] An example given earlier by Ricoeur of an agent accepting responsibility for something he/she did not do is a pet owner. One often forgets to put a leash on the dog . . . .

# 8 Consciousness and the self

At the outset, I would like to say that this chapter is not devoted to an analysis of consciousness per se. Such an analysis would, undoubtedly, include a description of the relationship existing between consciousness and the physical substratum giving rise to or serving as the ground of consciousness. This relationship has generated its own corpus of literature, and as yet, no description that is accepted by a majority of philosophers working in this area has emerged. For the purposes of this essay, I am simply going to assume that consciousness exists regardless of how it is related to the brain. Nor will I attempt a definition of the term 'consciousness'. I will simply lay down some verbal indications and/or examples of what I think the term means. Consciousness, a mental state, occurs when a human or animal is 'aware', through perception, of the existence of an external object, and when a human or animal is aware of some other mental or bodily state occurring to the subject. Thus, one can be conscious of cats, airplanes, etc., but also of sensations, feelings, emotions, beliefs, doubts, etc. I can only hope that the preceding provokes or stimulates a sympathetic reaction on the part of the reader because it is obvious that the term 'aware' or 'awareness' may simply be a synonym of 'conscious' or 'consciousness', and the preceding verbal attempt to characterize consciousness if treated as a definition would be circular.

To compound the problem, I would like to suggest that a being can also be 'conscious' without being 'aware'. (Some philosophers may want to reverse these terms.) That is to say, all of us have had the rather common everyday experience of driving down a highway safely (indicating that we were able to avoid obstacles and to remain on the roadbed) for miles on end and not be able to describe the vehicles encountered or passed because we were engaged in an interesting discussion, or mentally computing our personal finances, etc. Thus, we were sufficiently conscious in respect to our environment to maintain our survival but were not really *aware* of the environment at a cognitive level.

For the phenomenologists and for many analytic philosophers, for a being to be conscious involves being in a state of 'intentionality'. Intentionality (in this context as opposed to that of purposive activity) is the state in which a creature's attention is directed toward something – an object that can be either physical or mental. One's awareness is 'about something'. To repeat the old slogan coming from the literature of phenomenology, 'To be conscious is to be conscious of something'. This slogan is attributed to Franz Brentano and was supported vigorously by Edmund Husserl. Intentionality is often treated as being the mark of the mental as opposed to the non-mental. As I am writing these sentences, I am conscious or aware not only of the thoughts (mental events) that I want to convey through these words but also of the black marks falling upon a white surface (actually of dark purple marks appearing upon the green surface of a monitor) that serve as a medium by which my thoughts are conveyed. Whether or not cognitive scientists (including psychologists, neurophysiologists, and philosophers) have a difficult time explaining (and in some cases discussing the very existence of) consciousness relative to its physical ground is beside the point here.

Phenomenologically, I am aware of my present state of consciousness, and for someone else to declare that I am not so presently constituted suggests from my point of view that the theoretician making the claim is extremely presumptuous, or that the theoretician and I are not talking about the same thing.[1] I will put the best construction on this situation and assume that the latter is the case. The theoretician denying the existence of consciousness may have the same kind of experiences I do – viz., conscious experiences – but chooses to describe them in ways that do not imply the existence of certain characteristics that have been traditionally linked to the term 'awareness'. If this is an accurate description of the difference existing between my phenomenological approach to consciousness and the eliminativist's approach, then it can be assumed by the reader that the subsequent discussion will be based on the approach that is loosely labeled as phenomenological. However, at this time, I am more interested in ascertaining the relationship between a person's consciousness and that person's self.

I believe that Ricoeur's exposition of the self suffered from not having included an analysis of the relationship between the self and consciousness. Since Ricoeur did not differentiate between the two, I am not sure that he sees a difference between them. But, there is such a distinction, and if it is not made clear that self and consciousness should be distinguished, then difficulties, including a problem of circularity, come to the fore.

What kind of relationship between consciousness and self is needed to do justice to our concept of the self as 'character', or 'narrative identity', or as a trope supervenient on a family of subvenient properties? It has to be of a sort that connects the dynamic, temporal aspect of the person with a relatively stable set of properties or characteristics to which other properties may be added or subtracted that provide us with a picture or pattern of a person who is social as well as an individual in his/her qualities. The dynamic temporal aspect of the person is that which allows the narrative identity to unfold in time while the stable pattern, the character of the person, is that which allows for reidentification in time. If we treat consciousness as the dynamic aspect and the self as pattern or character, then these two aspects of the person can be conceived as interdependent. Consciousness without the self takes on the guise of pure spontaneity, and the self without consciousness takes on the appearance of a static entity. In order to show the interdependence of the two aspects of the person, it is helpful to look at Mead once again and at Sartre.

Mitchell Aboulafia has done us the service of comparing both Mead's and Sartre's (very important) work on consciousness and self. Aboulafia's conclusion is that both Mead's and Sartre's works individually are inadequate, but each can mutually correct the other's deficiency. (I will use Aboulafia's analysis but qualify it with my own.) In the case of Mead, his understanding of the self as 'I' and 'me' is extremely helpful in its emphasis upon the self's social roots and its connection to the social. Mead's attempt to give a genesis of the self based upon the ability of the individual to view him/herself from the perspective of the other is important in an affirmative sense as opposed to Sartre's analysis of the objectification of the self by the other's 'look.' Sartre's interpretation of the self as realizing itself as the object of the other's look treats the experience as basically confrontational or aggressive in content.

In contrast, Mead understands the self and, in particular, the 'me' aspect of the self, as manifesting a readiness to appropriate the values and attitudes of the society in which the self finds itself. The very beginning of the generation of the self (whether we agree that this is something that we can even get at is moot, but Mead's description could be treated as pertaining to the 'structure' of the self rather than of the origin of the self) is described as a lesson in cooperation between the individual and others. This is so because the linguistic element, the appropriation and use of symbols, demands interdependence and reciprocity between individuals before a symbol can even be used to designate oneself:

> For Mead, becoming an object-self involves considerably more than being looked-at by an other. I must learn to respond to myself through the verbal gesture; I must then go on to take the role of the other and

generalize other(s). In so doing, I come to view myself (without the empirical presence of the other) from various perspectives; I come to be both subject and object to myself.[2]

However, there is a difficulty with Mead's account of the self even though it has the desirable quality of bringing the social aspects of the self into play. This defect in Mead's approach (which I will treat presently) allows us, following Aboulafia here, to see the beneficial side of Sartre's treatment of consciousness.[3]

Sartre's analysis of the 'look' of the other that has a confrontational tonality about it was developed by Sartre in order to keep the spontaneity and the freedom of the consciousness of the individual intact and not allow an 'internalization' of the other.

Now, if this maintenance of freedom and spontaneity were all there is to the suggested improvement of Mead's analysis via Sartre, then it seems unnecessary because Mead's 'I' aspect of the self already is a seat of spontaneity and novelty, not to mention that it is the 'I-self' that has the ability to call into question and/or reject certain features of its society. The 'I' criticizes with an eye to developing an even better society. However, Mead's 'I' never has a sense of self running concurrently with its novel or spontaneous acts, and it is at this point that Sartre's understanding of consciousness can improve Mead's model.

In Mead's approach, the 'I' never has an awareness of itself in an immediate sense. The 'I' can only know the 'I' as already having been the case, which, of course, converts it into one of the static aspects of the 'me-self.' But, then the 'I' aspect becomes a surd to the self:

> To know the 'I' is impossible, for one can only know the 'me,' that the 'I' becomes as the object of another 'I,' as the stream of consciousness moves on. As soon as the 'I' is observed, it has already lost its status as an 'I' and becomes a 'me.' The person, as a composite of 'I' and 'me,' is caught in a dualism that leads to an infinite regress regarding self-knowledge.[4]

What this indicates, then, is that the 'I-self' is absorbed by the 'me-self' and no true freedom or spontaneity is available for the self:

> If there is a unity to the self, it is the unity of a 'thing', of an object, albeit a very complex object. If there is spontaneity, it is a spontaneity that happens to the self, for the person may contain a pole of novelty, but the self does not and cannot. The self, it seems, cannot shape its own destiny. It is not free to rebel against its own past.[5]

130

In contrast, Sartre's consciousness at a 'pre-reflective' level does have a 'sense of self' that does not totally turn the self into an object as is the case with Mead's 'I':

> For Sartre, consciousness is first and foremost pre-reflective; it is aware of objects and experiences itself as aware of these objects, but it does not experience itself as an object. A waiter can be aware of performing the duties of a waiter without reflecting on or making herself or himself an object (of study) – that is, without reflecting on or thinking about his or her identity as a waiter. As such, he or she has a pre-reflective consciousness of being a waiter, although he or she is also in a certain sense distant from being a waiter, because consciousness is not that of which it is aware.[6]

At the same time, there is always the danger of an 'impure reflection' taking place which is the attempt by consciousness to objectify psychic events.

However, consciousness on the pre-reflective level retains both freedom and a sense of self. Now, at this point, it is important to notice that Sartre's model also allows for the incorporation of temporality into the very nature of consciousness. In order for consciousness to be operative as consciousness, there must be a continual negating of that which it is not, viz., the object of consciousness, and at the same time, there is a self-nihilation of consciousness that allows it to be aware of itself.[7] This action of self-nihilation is temporal in that it must take time for the nihilation to take place, and, thus allow for self-awareness to be realized:

> Consciousness is ekstatic. This means not only that it is dispersed through time, but that it finds itself aware because it separates from itself and is thus thoroughly temporal. The nothing, consciousness, that allows the object to appear while not being it, is precisely the same nothing that becomes temporality in the activity of what Sartre calls *nihilation*, that is, negation.[8]

Not only is consciousness temporal in this sense (of self-nihilation and self-awareness), but it is also temporal in its stretch toward the future. In its self-nihilation, consciousness becomes aware not only of what it is but of what it is not, viz., its possibilities.

> The awareness of possibilities defines what one is in terms of what one is not, what one lacks. That which one lacks gives rise to one's sense of self. I become aware of myself as that which lacks $x$, $y$, or $z$. Further,

this lack, this not being or having $x$, $y$, or $z$, relates the pre-reflective self to itself as that which can choose $x$, $y$, or $z$.[9]

This integration of temporality and consciousness is extremely important to an appropriate understanding of the dynamics of the self as I understand the self, i.e., in terms of both the reidentification of the self (personal identity) and the person conceived as temporal.

As Aboulafia sees it, then, both Mead's and Sartre's model of the self have affirmative aspects as well as deficiencies. Aboulafia proposes that the affirmative aspects of both models should be brought together. For a coherent model of the self to emerge from this attempted synthesis, he has to show that the social structure of the self as understood by Mead is compatible with the self-nihilating and self-awareness aspects of the pre-reflective consciousness as developed by Sartre. The function of the self that allows such a merger is the self's ability to 'determine' itself. Aboulafia believes that Mead's development of the self as coming through role-playing should be supplemented (and essentially so) by the negations that Sartre sees employed by consciousness in its contact with the other.

Aboulafia's synthesis of these two models of the self takes the form of a genetic analysis of the role of negations in the development of the self's 'sense of self'. This genetic analysis is also based on a Freudian use of parents and authority figures as they lay down prohibitions for the infant and the child. Rather than re-presenting in detail Aboulafia's account of the self's journey to self-awareness through Freudian concepts, let me quickly indicate that the child's internalization of the external 'no' is part of the child's capacity to appropriate the role of the other as outlined by Mead. That is, Aboulafia deftly welds together the Sartrean conflict with the other with Mead's understanding of the self's development as coming through the individual's contact with the other in terms of role-playing.[10]

The sense of self that is given through this process of identification with others and through the ability to say 'No' to others and oneself is essential in order for one to have the capacity of self-determination. (I would use the term 'self-constitution'.) In order for the self to direct its activities, it needs a sense of *what* is being directed. Identification with others in terms of both role-playing and the use of nihilation does not provide enough content for the self to be self-determining. What more is needed, according to Aboulafia, is another element also provided by Mead's work, viz., 'sociality'. According to Mead, sociality is the ability of an organism to survive the transition from one social system to another:

> Sociality tells us that there is a betwixt-and-between systems in which a novel occurrence brings forth a readjustment in the system it affects, so

that a new system arises. The novel makes us reinterpret what has been because we then view the past in light of the present new system.[11]

For Mead, it is sociality that allows the organism or the self to be ready to encounter the novel or unexpected. The self through the ability of sociality, then, is deeply involved in the process of nihilation. In moving from the old system to the new, the self has to be aware of what is no longer the case and also what is coming into present existence. The self then learns to expect the what is not:

> The organism must become habituated to both being itself and not being itself, to being both object-self and other, if the organism is to adapt itself to the human condition. The consciousness of limit, the awareness of the (internal) non-being of oneself that is required for a fully realized sense of self, develops in part from the repeated challenge to the organism to integrate what it does not expect to be part of itself with itself.[12]

At this point, then, in respect to self-determination, Aboulafia is in a position to weld the insights of Mead and Sartre.

In this discussion, I am focusing on Aboulafia's analysis rather than specifically upon Sartre's because Aboulafia has taken the insights of both Mead and Sartre and put together a more accurate interpretation of the nature of the self in respect to self-determination. Mead provides a more sanguine picture of the self in its interaction with other selves. Mead emphasizes the cooperative nature of community in contrast to Sartre's emphasis upon the confrontational. On the other hand, Sartre's interpretation of consciousness is more profound than that of Mead. Even so, Sartre's description of the relationship between the pre-reflective and reflective consciousness is reversed by Aboulafia. Sartre says,

> [R]eflection has no kind of primacy over the consciousness reflected-on. It is not reflection which reveals the consciousness reflected-on to itself. Quite the contrary, it is the non-reflective consciousness which renders the reflection possible; there is a pre-reflective cogito which is the condition of the Cartesian cogito.[13]

Instead of agreeing with Sartre that the reflective consciousness is derived from the pre-reflective, Aboulafia asserts that it is the other way around. The pre-reflective is derived from the reflective:

It is only by becoming other to oneself through social interaction that one can become aware of (object-) self and other(ness), and until one has this awareness, it is not possible to speak of the lack that comes to inhabit pre-reflective consciousness (unless one wants to presume a magical nothingness as the definition of consciousness).[14]

I believe that Aboulafia is convincing in his understanding of the structure of the reflective and pre-reflective consciousness. The parenthetical statement in the preceding quotation indicates Aboulafia's rejection of the Sartrean interpretation of consciousness as a kind of 'spontaneous "nothing"',[15] or surd in the fabric of rationality.

However, Aboulafia is well aware of the reason why Sartre treated consciousness as nothingness, viz., as such it is the source of the radical freedom espoused by the early Sartre. Aboulafia respects this concern for the freedom of the self, but at the same time he is very much aware of his own use of Freud in his analysis of the self. And, traditionally, Freud has been used as an example of the deterministic point of view in respect to human choice.

Basically, Aboulafia reconciles the tension between determinism and freedom of choice in respect to the self's self-determination through the concept of sociality provided by Mead. Free choice is not an option, but being totally determined by prior sets of conditions or circumstances is not the case either:

> On the one hand, one can only be self-determined in the context of what one has been, and it would be an act of ignorance or bad faith to deny the facticity of the object-self. On the other hand, once one becomes aware of one's relationship to the other, to the novel, to living in sociality, as well as of the power of the negative (which one has internalized and which resides in consciousness), one can act to negate aspects of the not-self, and in altering them, thereby alter the horizon of one's self.[16]

Sociality takes into consideration the facticity, the giveness of the past, and to be self-determined means that one must work with what one has received and what one has become. Self-determination is not pure spontaneity. To take a direction is to start from somewhere. The self has the ability 'to adjust a limit of the self by negating the not-self . . . . One is not simply a thing, an in-itself, but an open system living in sociality'.[17] As a summarizing statement of Aboulafia's position on self-determination, the following is instructive:

> The capacity for self-determination emerges in the context of sociality, entails the internalization of the no, and comes to fruition when I am

sufficiently aware of the object-self and not-self to be able to say that this possible integration of the me and not-me is the me to come; it is the lack I experience now that must, and can, be overcome.[18]

However, the question of self-determination or self-constitution gives rise to a very serious problem, viz., the problem of circularity. The question is: Does Aboulafia's melding of the models of Mead and Sartre overcome this problem?

In order to address this question, let us turn to Robert Nozick's treatment of the self in his work *Philosophical Explanations*. In the section entitled 'Reflexivity', Nozick treats the problem of the indexical term 'I's ability to refer to the producer of the token 'I'. Nozick mentions several of the problems associated with the use of the term 'I'. However, for our purposes it is enough to indicate that the subject's ability to have self-knowledge is not explicated by its ability to use the term 'I', according to Nozick:

> If I always knew something of myself via a term or referring token, there would be needed the additional (unexplained) fact of my knowing the term referred to me, of my knowing I was its producer. Therefore, it seems we each must have a kind of access to ourselves which is not via a term or referring expression, not via knowing that a term holds true (of something or other).[19]

And, this 'access' other than through the reflexive capacity of the 'I' must be a kind of knowledge by acquaintance rather than by description. However, Nozick points out that it must be a kind of acquaintance different from the kind associated with knowing an object.[20]

Ultimately, Nozick concludes that self-knowledge is a 'basic phenomenon':

> Uniquely, selves know themselves in virtue of being identical with themselves, and this basic property of selves cannot be further explained. (I take eastern theories of 'non-dual consciousness' to fit this category.) The question, 'What is it about selves in virtue of which they have reflexive knowledge merely in virtue of the self-identity in which everything stands to itself?' would be a question without any answer. The phenomenon would be a basic phenomenon; it would be a brute fact that some things have it and others do not.[21]

Nevertheless, the problem of circularity emerges at this point. If the 'self' refers to itself in its capacity for self-knowledge, then

[s]till, how does it know it is referring to itself, in what does this knowledge consist? How does the self, placed inside the sentence or thought-frame, know that it itself is what is there?[22]

This problem is reminiscent of Sartre's concern for and rejection of the *transcendental* ego. If you recall, there is no ego standing behind consciousness for Sartre:

> [T]he phenomenological conception of consciousness renders the unifying and individualizing role of the *I* totally useless. It is consciousness, on the contrary, which makes possible the unity and the personality of my *I*. The transcendental *I*, therefore, has no *raison d'etre*.[23]

Sartre's consciousness, even though in itself [it is] 'nothing', has in its pre-reflective mode a 'sense of self' that is not a full-fledged 'impure' type of reflection. So, there is a distinction within Sartre's treatment of consciousness between the self as consciousness and the self as *transcendent* (I am not referring to the transcendental ego here). Also, in Aboulafia's treatment of Mead's 'I-self' and the 'me-self', Aboulafia seems to associate a kind of Sartrean consciousness with the 'I-self', and the 'me-self' seems to be analogous to the transcendent ego of Sartre.

In both Sartre's and Mead's treatment of the distinction occurring within the self, the conscious aspect also bears a self-awareness. The pre-reflective consciousness has an inchoate awareness that it belongs to *this* self, and the 'I-self' has an awareness that it is associated with *this* particular 'me-self'.

In contrast, Nozick (at least on the surface) makes no claim about distinctions within the self. Instead, he tries to make a case ('hesitantly') for the self's 'reflexive self-awareness' on the basis of its ability to 'synthesize' itself.[24] He realizes that there are problems existing with a 'preexisting I', and so he proposes instead that the self is formed in the very act of the reflexive act of the self.[25] Now, Nozick raises the question whether the self positing itself in the reflexive act itself is always a new creation. This question is based on Nozick's reluctance to let go of the 'preexisting self' in its entirety:

> Can we say (afterwards) that what did A(0) was the entity E which A(0) itself synthesized? Can the rabbit be pulled out of the rabbit? It is some such theory as this that Fichte presents; he speaks of the self as positing itself, also of the self positing itself as positing itself. (Is there a limit to how many levels up this qua must go?)[26]

136

Nozick's answer to the question of the rabbit being pulled from the rabbit is that the past syntheses of the self feed into the present self-synthesis. And not every self-synthesis in the present is a new creative act:

> Usually, the self habitually follows the earlier precedents, aligning itself with those precedents that can cover it most closely. Sometimes self-reference will occur more self-consciously, a self will step back from habit to consider its nature; on some occasions the self-reference may occur self-consciously, as a self-synthesis.[27]

Given this interpretation of self-synthesis (or self-constitution), it would appear that Nozick has, in fact, implicitly distinguished within the self two aspects to the self, i.e., 1) the self as having been synthesized in the past and feeding into the present synthesis and 2) the self as synthesizing. This implicit distinction seems to be parallel to either Sartre's or Mead's distinction. If my interpretation of Nozick's treatment of the self is correct, and if a problem of circularity attends the analysis of the self, then it most likely occurs at the point of a preexisting self or transcendental ego. None of the three thinkers (Sartre, Mead, and Nozick) posits one. In fact, they (especially in the cases of Sartre and Nozick) are very much opposed to the notion of a preexisting self.[28] With Nozick's attempt to describe the self-referring, self-synthesizing act of the self, I believe that one has done as much as can be done to get rid of the circularity of a self positing the self.

Certainly, if what is really basic is the phenomenon of the self being synthesized in an act of reflexive self-reference as opposed to a mere phenomenon of reflexive self-awareness, then Nozick, in essence, is claiming at a certain point that nothing further can be explained about the constitution of the self. That an entity can have this kind of self-reference and self-synthesis is simply a given, a brute fact. The question of vicious circularity can only be raised if the critic is unwilling to accept the notion of self-constitution (self-synthesis). Such unwillingness would most likely be due to an unwillingness to forsake the third-person point of view as certainly espoused by Dennett and others.[29]

Given Nozick's understanding of the self as a self-synthesizer, he raises the question of the self's unity over time because the self as depicted so far could just as easily be a Humean bundle as an integrated entity. In response to this question, Nozick engages in a mereology that I do not think is particularly helpful nor does he come to a satisfactory conclusion as to how the whole self can be unified relative to its parts. What is important here is Nozick's attitude toward the self as being unified, because it strikes me that he is taking a phenomenological approach:

I do not need any convincing that there is unity; what I need is to understand how unity is possible. If I need a transcendental argument, it is not one that starts with other things and reaches unity as a condition of their possibility; it is one that starts with unity and delves to the conditions of *its* possibility.[30]

Nozick makes a comment that suggests support for my view of the self as a supervenient property:

Unity can be an emergent property, based upon parts without unity of their own. The unity of X consists of X's integrity at its own level. It has this integrity provided its identity is not reducible to that of its parts; there are not parts of X such that X's identity over time is equivalent to the sum of the identities over time of these parts. This formulation does not assume that the parts themselves have unity or that there are any proper parts. Something is a unity, whether by its metaphysical nature or as carved out, if its identity over time is not equivalent to the sum of identities over time of proper parts it may have. No underlying unity is presupposed. Unity sometimes does arise from an underlying unity; but the picture that unity can arise only out of unity no longer grips us.[31]

Of course, the term 'emergent' has had the connotation in the past of not only referring to an entity (or level of scientific investigation) that arises from lower levels but also that the emergent entity has causal properties that are not simply reducible to the causal properties of the lower level from which it arose.

The term 'supervenient', however, never 'forgets' its roots. That is to say, when a property is supervenient on another property or set of properties, the former's causal capacity is always dependent upon the latter's. If Nozick's understanding of 'emergent' could conform to my understanding of 'supervenient', then his help would be greatly appreciated. It seems to me that given Nozick's understanding of the self synthesizing itself in light of its past syntheses, then the self is not really 'emergent' in the sense of the autonomy suggested by that term. But, in fact, the self is supervenient upon the body and psychological qualities.

Besides Nozick's apparent support for my position on the emergent-supervenient concept, he also provides support in still yet another metaphysical sense; i.e., I treat the self as a property or an abstract particular, and Nozick also suggests that one could conceivably treat the self as a property. Unfortunately, he has a failure of nerve and backs off from the self as property even after finding it a helpful concept in dealing with 'some well-known perplexities'.[32]

One such perplexity is Hume's problem, viz., whenever Hume entered into himself he never discovered the self as an object but only stumbled across certain perceptions. 'If the self were a property, we would expect Hume's quest to have had its result, for the self could not then be found as an object of introspective search.'[33] (I am not sure, though, why the self treated as a trope could not be introspected. Can we not discern aspects of our character, for example, through introspection?) Treating the self as a property also is helpful in understanding why one is reluctant 'to imagine the self apart from any embodiment or realization'.[34] Further, Nozick indicates that on 'an Aristotelian view of a property as existing in the entities that possess it . . . we would understand why the self must be instantiated in some stuff, however wispy'.[35]

In respect to this second perplexity, the difference between my view of the self as supervenient property and Nozick's view is that I do not view the self as 'instantiated in' something because 1) this approach suggests that the body per se realizes the self, and 2) as a trope the self is a particular and as such cannot be instantiated in the traditional sense. Rather, the self as a supervenient property is realized by certain physical *and* psychological properties of an individual. Yet, the physical is absolutely necessary for the self to be realized superveniently just as it is necessary for the physical to be present in order for the self to be 'embodied' in Nozick's sense. But, given his earlier suggestion that the self is 'emergent', would not the relation between self and body be better understood as supervenience rather than as 'embodiment'?

The third perplexity mentioned by Nozick is related to the problem of 'embodiment' as indicated in the second perplexity. That is to say, it is difficult for Nozick

> to see how the self can be identical with any particular stuff, or even to see how the self is connected with that stuff, whether it be matter or wispier material (for example, ethereal 'bodies').[36]

Nozick goes on to indicate that it is difficult in general to ascertain what the relationship between a property and the object that instantiates the property really is, but this is not restricted to the body-self relationship. And, it may be the case that the body-self relationship may shed light, in general, on the relationship existing between objects and the properties instantiated by them. Again, it seems to me that this third perplexity is less severe if treated as I have above, i.e., on the view that the self is a supervenient abstract particular. Certainly, the self as an abstract particular supervenient upon both the physical and psychological properties, or as the narrative identity, of the individual does not involve us in the problem of 'where' is the property in the instantiating object or how much of the 'stuff' of the instantiating object is needed to insure the instantiation of the property, etc., any more than one asks 'Where is the *badness?*' in a moral situation such as an armed robbery and murder. Of course, I am not claiming that spatial location in respect to either the self or moral properties is irrelevant. The 'badness' in respect to the robbery taking place in Dubuque cannot simply 'float.' It is where the robbery is, but you cannot pick it out in the same way you would pick out blood, a weapon, etc.

In spite of the three perplexities being less severe if we treat the self as a property, Nozick backs off from endorsing this view even though he admits that this approach may shed light on old problems. Here is his statement disavowing his support of this understanding of the self:

> Yet, in this instance I do not find the view of the self as a property sufficiently illuminating, clarifying, and fruitful in its consequences to put it forth, except as a curiosity, despite its explaining why certain puzzles about the self have arisen, and despite its providing some enduring entity for the self to be. The view seems too much like a bit of philosophical chicanery, too much froth and too little substance.[37]

I suspect that the 'too much froth' and 'too little substance' is based on a reluctance to leave behind the third person point of view paradigm and the position of treating properties as universals.

I have nothing against a 'conservative approach' in these matters as a methodological tool. By a 'conservative approach', I mean an approach that takes seriously Occam's Razor and, therefore, is likely to be reductive in type. I agree that entities should not be multiplied willy-nilly. I agree that 'mysterious stuff' should not close the door to further investigation and discussion. However, on the other hand, I see no good reason to delay generating an interpretive theory about certain phenomena until the scientists are in a position to speak authoritatively on the topic in question. Terms (and/or concepts) such as 'self' and 'personal identity' have functions, applications, in everyday life. To ascertain what self and personal identity are is certainly an appropriate intellectual endeavor in spite of the fact that not all of the information or data are in hand in respect to the phenomena in question. When P.M. Churchland and Dennett suggest that certain 'folk' terms and/or concepts will some day be explicable in scientifically acceptable terminology, they may well be correct. But to intimate that, until that time arrives, attempts to shed light on the nature of the phenomena in terms that they believe belong to the province of 'folk psychology' or any other alleged 'folk tales,' etc., and are therefore misguided is simply not correct.

In the first place, their scientifically acceptable theories, concepts, and terms are not necessarily free from metaphorical or anthropomorphic undertones. Terms such as 'mind', 'self', 'personal identity', and 'supervenience' may ultimately still serve in a scientifically appropriate manner even though some of the earlier connotations associated with these terms may drop away. These 'folk' terms may well become dead metaphors, and thereby, scientifically respectable.

Another reason not to wait upon the advance of science in respect to some of the so-called 'folk' concepts and terms is the moral, valuational, social, and political implications of the terms 'self', 'personal identity', and 'mind'. If concepts such as supervenience and/or narrative identity can shed light for us in the present day upon the social and political nature of persons, then we do not have to wait for the imprimatur of science in order to continue this kind of analysis. If one realizes that Mead's 'self' has no meaning outside the context of society or that Ricoeur's narrative identity has no relevance apart from moral and ethical implications, then this is enlightening in its own right.

Thus, Nozick's failure of nerve in respect to endorsing the concept of the self as property is unfortunate, given the ebb and flow of the philosophical endeavor. If a concept helps clarify some perplexities, then it should be evaluated and not merely dismissed as froth or of little substance.

In the following chapter, I call into question Derek Parfit's use of thought experiments in his analysis of personal identity. The problem, as I see it, is not that Parfit uses technology to call into question the concept of personal identity, but rather that he misuses it when doing so. In the process, he gives false support to a reductionistic approach to the self and personal identity.

## Notes

[1]    See Daniel C. Dennett, C. Three, 'A Visit to the Phenomenological Garden', *Consciousness Explained* (Boston: Little, Brown, and Company, 1991).

[2]    Aboulafia, 54.

[3]    For a critique of the Sartrean view of consciousness see Laird Addis, *Natural Signs: A Theory of Intentionality* (Philadelphia: Temple University Press, 1989, 48-49.

[4]    Ibid., 57.

[5]    Ibid.

[6]    Ibid., 31-32.

[7]    Ibid., 30.

8   Ibid.

9   Aboulafia, 59.

10  Ibid., 84-101.

11  Ibid., 61-62.

12  Ibid., 94-95.

13  Jean-Paul Sartre, *Being and Nothingness* (New York: Philosophical Library, 1956), liii.

14  Aboulafia, 95.

15  Ibid., 124.

16  Ibid., 100.

17  Ibid.

18  Ibid., 101.

19  Robert Nozick, *Philosophical Explanations* (Cambridge, Mass: Harvard University Press, 1981), 81.

20  Ibid.

21  Ibid., 82.

22  Ibid., 83.

23  Jean-Paul Sartre, *The Transcendence of the Ego* (New York: Hill and Wang, 1990), 40.

24  Nozick, 87.

25  Ibid.

26  Ibid., 89.

27  Ibid.

28  Ibid., 92.

29  Daniel C. Dennett, *The Intentional Stance* (Cambridge, Mass.: The MIT Press, 1987), 3-11.

30  Nozick, 98.

31  Ibid., 100.

32  Ibid., 111.

33  Ibid.

34  Ibid.

35  Ibid.

36  Ibid., 111-112

37  Ibid., 114.

# 9 A major problem with Parfit

Although concern with the problem of personal identity in the contemporary period certainly antedated the work of Derek Parfit, it is Parfit's article 'Personal Identity', published in 1971, along with his book *Reasons and Persons*, published in 1984, that has given great impetus to a large body of work during the last twenty years. Much of the interest of Parfit's work on this topic is due to his use of thought experiments that employ imaginative technological variations on the physical and psychological properties of human beings in order to determine what it is about personal identity that is important to the human being. Harold Noonan in *Personal Identity* suggests that Parfit tries to cast doubt on the 'only x and y' principle by the use of thought experiments. This principle

> asserts that whether a certain later person P2 is identical with a certain earlier person P1 can depend only on facts about P2 and P1 and the intrinsic relationships between them; no facts about individuals other than P2 and P1 can be relevant to whether P2 is the same person as P1.[1]

Parfit's thought experiments feature fission of the brain with the severed hemispheres being placed in two different cranial cavities and 'teletransportation' of a person from one planet to another via replication of the person's body, with different kinds of scenarios all designed to call the concept of personal identity into question. Through our responses to these variations on the same theme, Parfit asks us to believe that what matters is not the literal endurance of a person through time, but rather, as Noonan puts it, 'a Parfitian survival', i.e., that only psychological connectedness/continuity in the 'widest sense' 'deserves to be regarded as what really matters in survival'.[2]

Parfit arrives at this conclusion by his observations that if you are a person fearing the fission of your brain, then it would be irrational for you to treat that possible event as being as serious as the event of your death.[3] Parfit then declares that if we have an interest in our literal survival, then that must be a derived interest – derived from a Parfitian-type survival.[4] Noonan argues that Parfit's argument is 'inconclusive' in that

> it establishes that one cannot *both* regard personal identity as something which is of non-derivative importance *and* regard it as determinable by extrinsic facts, but it gives no reason why one should not retain the common-sense view that personal identity is *both* of non-derivative importance *and* intrinsically determined.[5]

Noonan argues that the commonsense view that personal identity is non-derivative and intrinsically determined can be maintained in the face of thought experiments involving fission if one allows for a 'Multiple Occupancy Thesis' –

> that two or more persons may be at a given time the co-occupants of a certain body and the joint thinkers of certain thoughts. But whilst the Multiple Occupancy Thesis is undeniably counter-intuitive, it is certainly no more counter-intuitive than Parfit's thesis.[6]

This tactic on the part of Noonan is supposed to erase the perplexity we supposedly feel upon hearing about Parfit's fission cases. For example, if one's hemispheres are separated and placed in two different cranial cavities, then does one continue as two persons? If one were to so continue, then the 'only x and y' principle (the notion that personal identity demands unity) is violated. But, on the other hand, if one of the two hemispheres in its new bearer is destroyed, then a person's identity seems to be preserved in the remaining hemisphere. Thus, a conundrum arises. If one of the two separated hemispheres (call it 'A') is destroyed and hemisphere 'B' survives, then personal identity is preserved. However, if both hemispheres remain viable, then identity is lost even though B in the latter case is no different from B in the former case.

The conundrum turns on one's acceptance of extrinsic relations as making a difference to personal identity and upon a non-derivative notion of personal identity as being contributed by *literal* survival. Parfit, of course, opts for denying the second conjunct. Noonan opts for intrinsic relations as holding between the unfissioned brain and its two fissioned successors but at the cost of having two persons with each having its own identity occupying one and the same cranial cavity prior to fission.

Both Parfit's and Noonan's positions on the notion of personal identity are hardly acceptable. As I see it, the problem lies in that both accept the same premise, viz., that the two hemispheres of one's brain are similar to each other in every way prior to fission. There is sufficient evidence from psychological experimentation presently available to show that the left and right hemispheres have different functions in most individuals. At this point, there is no need to list the respective functions in each case nor is there any point in presenting statistics on the minority percentage of individuals that could serve as a counter-instance to the general rule that the hemispheres are dissimilar in function (and thereby serve as evidence of the credibility of fission). The point that I am making here is that these two individuals have allowed the method of thought experimentation to overextend itself.

The overextension of the use of thought experiments in respect to 'fission' occurs not in respect to the imaginative technique of severing the corpus callosum nor in the notion of transplanting the hemispheres. (Even though the technical aspects of 'hooking up' the hemispheres to the appropriate afferent and efferent pathways is mind-boggling in its complexity.) The problem lies in what was indicated in the last paragraph, viz., the assumption that both hemispheres are identical in their cognitive, mnemonic, and affective capacities and, furthermore, that the hemispheres, even before being separated from one another, have little or no interdependent functions.

Until the autonomous nature of each hemisphere is clearly established, thought experiments depending on commissurotomy are piling 'what ifs(2)' upon 'what ifs(1)'. 'What ifs(1)' would be the notion that the functions of one hemisphere are identical to those of its cranial mate, and the 'what ifs(2)' would be the highly improbable successful transplantings.

What I am contending is supported by Kathleen V. Wilkes in *Real People*. In this work, Wilkes argues that one of the major differences in the use of thought experiments in science as contrasted with their use in philosophy is that in the former instance, a scientist tends to be rigorous in giving the 'background conditions against which he sets his experiment':[7]

> The reason for that is simple and obvious: experiments, typically, set out to show what difference some factor makes; in order to test this, other relevant conditions must be held constant, and the problematic factor juggled against that constant background. If several factors were all fluctuating, then we would not know which of them (or which combination of them) to hold responsible for the outcome. . . . As far as is possible, then, the relevant *ceteris paribus* conditions are either

stated, or assumed.[8]

Wilkes refers to Einstein's thought experiment in which he imagines himself taken to the speed of light. In this thought experiment, Einstein suspends only one of the relevant features belonging to the context of particles and the speed of light, viz., that particles significantly larger than photons *cannot* attain the speed of light and then asks the question: What would a person see if he /she were able to attain the speed of light if Maxwell's theory of electrodynamics is correct? The answer is: a stationary oscillating field.[9] And, since such a field is impossible, questions were raised about Maxwell's theory. The point Wilkes is making is that thought experiments in natural science 'presuppose that all relevant background conditions are included and specified',[10] or at least they are presumed as remaining in effect as the experimenter focuses his/her attention hypothetically on varying the condition in question:

> Put another way, the 'possible world' is *our* world, the world described by our sciences, except for one distinguishing difference. So we know or can assume everything else that it is relevant to know, in order to assess that thought experiment.[11]

And,

> [l]egitimate thought experiments must spell out for us the (relevant) respects in which the 'possible world' does and does not differ from the actual world. In sharp contrast, what we find in the fantastical thought experiments [such as half-brain transplants] we have been considering is a virtual abandonment of any attempt to identify, restrict, or fix the *ceteris paribus* conditions.[12]

This requirement does not seem to be followed by the fission and teletransportation thought experiments generated by Parfit.

Do the fission experiments take into consideration the rather well-known differentiation of functions existing between the left and right hemispheres? If anything, a strong case has to be made in the cases of brain damage that the intact hemisphere can, in fact, pick up the duties formerly carried out by the damaged hemisphere. Some rehabilitation has been achieved in certain cases, but whether full reconstitution of functions usually carried out by the injured hemisphere can ever be attained is questionable. So, in the cases of 'fission', not only is the hypothetical severing of the hemispheres and their reinstallation in different cranial cavities the hypothetical variant, but the

146

supposed identity of functions such as memory, emotions, propositional attitudes in the form of dispositions, etc., existing between the two formerly connected hemispheres is also part of the hypothetical variant. But, then, what about the brainstem of the donor of the hemispheres? Can this be split in half to accompany the appropriate cortical hemisphere as it is deposited in a new body with no differentiation taking place between the two halves? And, of course, all of the preceding splitting, cleaving, and reinstalling presupposes that reattachment of the hemispheres and the severed portions of the brain stem to new spinal cords is possible without loss of function relative to neuronal circuitry.

The question becomes: Just how much of the thought experiment pertains to the separation of the hemispheres and how much involves all of the other components mentioned above as well? Where do the presumed background conditions begin and end in the case of fission?

These questions can be posed in respect to teletransportation experiments as well. Are we to assume in a 'replication' situation that the blueprint of my body (the body that was destroyed on earth) and is now being used on Mars to inform a 'mess' of flesh, bone, blood, etc. (not to mention that a genetic map has to be installed as well) is so accurate that the replica and I are 'both physically and psychologically . . . exactly similar'?[13] Just how is the pile of flesh, bone, blood, etc., that will be my replica *produced* so that it can receive my physical and psychological 'imprint'? To what extent does Parfit's teletransportation cases presume that one's molecular, atomic, and subatomic levels are *exactly* reproduced in the replica? And should they not be so reproduced so that the replica is exactly similar to the original? After all, who knows to what extent our personalities are dependent upon genetic factors (DNA) and to what extent they are dependent upon environmental factors?

The point, once again, is that thought experiments as used by Parfit are not sufficiently described so that one can ascertain what background conditions are being assumed. A defender of Parfit and, at the same time, a critic of Wilkes, Daniel Kolak, does not seem to grasp Wilkes' point. Kolak, in his article 'The Metaphysics and Metapsychology of Personal Identity' says,

> Consider the physicist's use of thought experiments involving frictionless surfaces. Although a true frictionless surface does not exist anywhere in nature, nor *could* such a surface exist, even in principle, physicists perform idealized thought experiments in which they manipulate imaginary hockey-pucks on an imaginary, frictionless surface. This idealization allows experimenters the luxury of leaving out all forces but the particular one they wish to single out and scrutinize.[14]

And he applies this concept to thought experiments in respect to personal identity: 'In thought experiments about persons, a properly imagined set-up allows us to leave out all factors but the one under examination'.[15] Obviously, Wilkes claims the opposite, i.e., the background conditions are not 'left out' of consideration, but a specific factor of the phenomenon in question is mentally altered or varied in order to shed light on the phenomenon as experienced.

Now, if we attempt to put the best construction on Kolak's remarks, he may mean by 'leave out all factors but the one under examination' that the thought experimenter focuses or concentrates on the factor being altered or varied. Even so, this construing of Kolak's intent is silent about the role of background conditions in thought experiments, thereby precluding a clear delineation between the factor(s) being altered mentally and the background conditions that remain unaltered.

Returning to Parfit's teletransportation experiment, I must repeat the question whether the 'fleshly stuff' of the replica is exactly similar to my genetic map? Further, will all of the positioning of the subatomic particles in the replica be exactly similar to that of my subatomic particles when the 'blueprint' was made (cf. Wilkes 42-43)? This rhetorical question is not simply a matter of splitting hairs on my part. Allow me to quote Kolak:

> None of the thought experiments personal identity theorists consider involve logical impossibilities. But neither do they involve physical impossibilities; they might *at present* be impossible to carry out technologically but do not break the known laws of nature. In this respect, thought experiments about persons require less of a conceptual leap than Einstein's.[16]

I am contending that Kolak is wrong about Parfit's thought experiments; they do in fact depend upon a breaking of 'the known laws of nature' (i.e., if we can ever be sure what a law of nature really is. See Chapter II of James Fetzer's *Philosophy of Science*.) Quantum mechanics tells us that we can never, with precision, know simultaneously the momentum and position of electrons. Yet, if the replica is to carry out *my* particular intentions and goals for the future, then perhaps there must be an exact positioning of the subatomic particles in question. Paradoxically, this requirement is in place if one accepts the notion held by some theorists working in the area of freedom of the will and determinism that the acausality needed as a basis for the capability of making 'real' choices is provided by Heisenberg's Principle of Indeterminacy applied to brain cells and/or neurotransmitters. (I personally do not subscribe to this defense of freedom of the will, but certainly it is reasonable to ask Kolak to respond to the problem it presents to his claim that Parfit's thought experiments do not break any laws of nature.) Of course, to claim that the replica will be constructed in such a way as to duplicate exactly all of the positioning of the subatomic particles pertinent to my framing a plan for my future is to violate the canon of quantum mechanics mentioned above. Such duplication could only be accidental and not by design. If we take the claims of the majority of theoretical physicists seriously, then the impossibility of our getting a precise reading of the position and momentum of the electrons relative to decision-making is not a matter of crude instrumentation *at present*. Rather, *in principle* it is the very nature of electrons to be indeterminate in respect to the properties mentioned.

If the preceding account is true of the 'laws' of quantum mechanics, and if it is also the case (as some defenders of freedom of the will advocate) that freedom of choice is dependent upon the spontaneous activity of subatomic particles in the brain, then Kolak's defense of Parfit's thought experimentation is wrong. The 'known laws of nature' are being 'broken' in the assumption that the replica can carry out in a non-accidental, mechanical way the intentions, goals, aspirations, and plans of the original me in a predictable manner according to the 'blueprint' taken of the original me prior to my destruction in the teletransportation process. If the replica does carry out the activities chosen by the original me for my future, it can only be coincidental, and, of course, nothing within the empirical posture would necessarily rule against this contingency. However, mere coincidence is not enough for us to identify the replica with the original me.

In Kolak's criticism of Wilkes' conservative approach to thought experiments, he chastises her with the following statement:

[W]e philosophers must be especially careful not to limit our understanding of 'realism' to what has been painted, and is paintable, on canvases deemed acceptable to hang in the *old* 'real' universe – that out-dated, classical gallery that got turned upside down and inside out by the advent of relativity theory and quantum mechanics. . . . [T]he universe of relativized spacetime, the uncertainty principle, vacuum fluctuations, superposition of states, black holes, wormholes, virtual particles, superstring theory, collapse of waves of probability into waves of actuality by consciousness – to name but a few of the more recent 'scientific sobrieties' – makes for new visions of personal identity a perfect gallery. In *this* newly strange universe there is more than enough room for the *realistic* picture of the metaphysical, metapsychological subject that some of us have only begun to paint.[17]

149

If my criticism in the preceding paragraph holds, then Kolak's admonishment of Wilkes has backfired upon him. One of the very elements in the litany he has presented us, viz., quantum mechanics, does not grant sufficient credibility to the teletransportation thought experiment so that if even we are supposed to settle for survival rather than full identity (one of the major thrusts of Parfit's program), we do not have enough assurance that there is a 'psychological connectedness' between the original me and the replica. Parfit admits that in the teletransportation case if one understands personal identity in terms of physical continuity, then I die even if the replica carries on my 'blueprint'.[18] However, even psychological continuity is lost if, in fact, such continuity is dependent upon physical factors as is believed to be the case by those advocates of freedom of the will that base choice upon the indeterminacy of electrons in the brain. Thus, the *decision* to carry out an intention would be directly dependent upon the indeterminate properties of the relevant electrons. However, Parfit says,

> Besides direct memories, there are several other kinds of direct psychological connection. One such connection is that which holds between an intention and the later act in which this intention is carried out.[19]

If, however, the decisions relative to carrying out intentions are governed by indeterminate subatomic particles in the brain and the attempt to replicate such is in principle impossible, then the teletransportation thought experiment, contrary to Kolak's general pronouncement about Parfit's thought experiments in respect to personal identity not violating the known laws of nature, is an even greater 'conceptual leap' than Einstein's experiment in respect to light.

Further, his list of scientific theories and principles that call into question the mechanical universe of Newton may or may not have any bearing upon the question of personal identity. At this point in the discussion about the problem of identifying whatever it is that constitutes the reason for many of us not giving up the concept of personal identity, it does not advance the discussion for Kolak simply to list areas of scientific endeavor that are *presently* puzzling or barely begun or mysterious for both the scientific investigator and lay person. Such puzzling areas of science in no way provide a conceptual license that legitimates an 'anything goes' attitude when it comes to investigating personal identity through the means of 'fantastical' thought experiments.[20]

I am not denying the importance of the role of thought experiments in either the construction of scientific hypotheses or in the analysis of concepts by philosophers. In fact, the role of narrative identity stressed by Paul Ricoeur could be considered a variation on the theme of thought experiments to the extent that fictional accounts of narrative identity (or the loss thereof) suggest to us what the essential aspects of selfhood might be. Ricoeur, however, points to some contrasts existing between 'the puzzling cases' of literary fiction and the thought experiments of Parfit. First, the very thing that Parfit varies in his thought experiments is the thing that the literary fictions retain as an invariant , viz., 'the corporeal condition assumed to constitute the unavoidable mediation between self and world'.[21] What is varied, instead, in the literary realm is the context of the corporeal nature of the literary character. Ricoeur is extremely doubtful that 'technological dreaming' in which the person is replaced by the brain can really be helpful in the analysis of personal identity:

> The real enigma is whether we are capable of conceiving of alternative possibilities within which corporeity as we know it, or enjoy it or suffer from it, could be taken as a variable, a contingent variable, and without having to transpose our earthly experiences in the very description of the case in question.[22]

Ricoeur also calls into question the lack of 'alterity' or the 'other' in Parfit's thought experiments. The experimental neurosurgeon and one's brain are the only principals involved. To the extent that one takes Dennett's six conditions of personhood seriously, in which, among other things, a human that can both take a moral posture toward other humans and also receive similar treatment from others is considered a human,[23] and to the extent that one treats Locke's understanding of the term 'person' as being 'forensic' in meaning, then Ricoeur's second concern is well-taken. Parfit's thought experiments seem to treat humans like 'pieces of meat' instead of being considered socially interactive and interdependent agents. Humans 'achieve' personhood not only on the basis of their monadic qualities but also on the basis of how they are received and understood by fellow humans. If this is true, then the discussion raised by the question of personal identity cannot be advanced by thought experiments that ignore the conditions that permit one to ascribe moral agency to a human. Of course, it is true that Parfit's primary reason for engaging in a discussion about the nature of personal identity is to shed light upon the moral responsibility one has toward his/her species' progeny. However, that is not to say that he has considered the possibility that an accurate interpretation of the concept of personal identity requires one to recognize that moral qualities are included in that concept.

Ricoeur believes that the most important difference between Parfit's thought experiments and literary fictions, however, is that the latter raise the question of the 'who' of the human raising the question of personal identity. Even in the 'puzzling' cases of literary fiction in which the hero experiences a 'loss of self', there is still something that raises the question of 'Who am I?' Parfit's emphasis upon mere survival does not address this phenomenon in an adequate manner:

> In a sense, there is a point at which we must be able to say, with Parfit: *identity is not what matters*. But it is still someone who says this. The sentence 'I am nothing' must be allowed to retain its paradoxical form: 'nothing' would no longer mean anything if it were not imputed to an 'I'. What is still 'I' when I say that it is nothing if not precisely a self deprived of assistance from sameness?[24]

For Ricoeur, it is narrative fictions that allow us to infer indirectly who we are as we take on the identity of a fictional character and discover whether there is a fit between ourselves and the character depicted. The obtaining of self-knowledge does not seem to be part of the outcome of one's entertaining a Parfitian thought experiment.

Roy Sorenson's concluding remarks in his book *Thought Experiments* indicate that one should treat thought experiments as being analogous to the use of the compass for navigation. The compass is not always foolproof (e.g., in the presence of magnets). It is useful even though many persons in the past and present had/have no idea of why it works. Likewise, in respect to thought experiments,

> they systematically err under certain conditions and so are best used with sensitivity to their foibles and limited scope. Thought experiments do not directly indicate the alethic status of propositions; they instead provide evidence about the conceivability of a proposition that only imperfectly corresponds to its possibility. This correspondence is close enough for most purposes. But under rare conditions, thought experiment leads us badly astray. . . . The circumspect thinker will use thought experiment as one technique among many, basing his final judgment on the *collective* behavior of his indicators.[25]

Sorenson's position seems eminently sensible. It is my belief that some persons writing in the area of personal identity have been far too smitten by Parfitian type thought experiments. Although this type of thought experiment can be helpful in providing us with an awareness of the nature of certain minimal conditions pertaining to personal identity, there is much more involved in the concepts of personhood and personal identity than is available in the analysis of fission, fusion, and replication. Concentrating too much effort on such experiments may mislead one into believing that if one addresses the problems raised by Parfit, then one has exhausted all that is pertinent to the question of personal identity. It is my hope that this essay will dispel such a notion.

## Notes

[1]  Noonan, 16.
[2]  Ibid., 194.
[3]  Ibid., 126.
[4]  Ibid., 194.
[5]  Ibid., 195-196.
[6]  Ibid., 197.
[7]  Kathleen Wilkes, *Real People* (Oxford: Clarendon Press, 1988), 7.
[8]  Ibid.
[9]  Ibid., 4.
[10]  Ibid., 9.
[11]  Ibid., 8.
[12]  Ibid., 45.
[13]  Derek Parfit, *Reasons*, 200.
[14]  Daniel Kolak, 'The Metaphysics and Metapsychology of Personal Identity', *American Philosophical Quarterly* 30.1 (January 1993): 46.
[15]  Ibid.
[16]  Ibid.
[17]  Ibid., 49.
[18]  Parfit 204.
[19]  Ibid., 205.
[20]  Wilkes, 46.
[21]  Paul Ricoeur, 'Narrative Identity', *On Paul Ricoeur* ed. David Wood (London: Routledge, 1991), 196.
[22]  Ibid., 197.
[23]  Daniel Dennett, 'Conditions of Personhood', *The Identities of Persons*, ed. Amelie Oksenberg Rorty (Berkeley: U. of California Press, 1976), 192.
[24]  Ricoeur, 'Narrative Identity', 199.
[25]  Roy A. Sorenson, *Thought Experiments* (New York: Oxford University Press, 1992), 289.

# 10 Conclusion

## The self as trope and the commonsensical notion of self-identity

A reasonable question arises at this point: Does the theory of the self outlined earlier have any resemblance or pertinence to the everyday notion of 'self-identity'? I believe that an affirmative response is appropriate. The common notion of self-identity often revolves around such questions as 'Who am I really?' or 'What can I do to fulfill myself?' or 'What should I become?' The last question should be understood as a plea for moral direction or as the initial step in a search for an appropriate style of life rather than as a request for vocational guidance. If the subject poses these questions to him/herself in a serious manner, then it seems likely that some form of intentional behavior will eventually occur based on the subject's evaluation of his/her options. In such an appraisal, the subject must consider who he or she happens to be in the present relative to the constraints and abilities developed in his/her past. To put it prosaically, before one can strike out in a new direction in life, one has to know one's present location. Taking stock of one's options in a realistic manner will involve, therefore, recognizing the salient features of one's own 'trope' or 'narrative identity'. So, yes, the theory of self presented earlier does seem to be harmonious with the everyday understanding of the search for self-realization.

Now, if we were to place ourselves in the position of deciding on some plan of action for self-realization, is it not the case that, as we run through some of our options relative to taking a new direction in life, we can decide rather quickly on those options that are 'realistic' for us and those that are not? It may be the case that some of us would make lists of our strong points and our weak points given the conditions of our present situation (geographical,

154

interpersonal, vocational, etc.) and how these conditions would change upon our exercising those options that we believe would cause a major change in our lifestyle. But, by and large, even those of us who engage in this kind of discursive activity already have a sense of 'fit' or commensurability between our present capacities (and liabilities) and the image of who we will become given our attempt to exercise new options. The point I am making is that the notion that the self is an abstract particular or trope is supported by the almost instantaneous awareness on our part of whether the projected self is a viable possibility based on our past and present self. Usually, we do not have to survey discrete memory units, arrange hierarchically our talents and abilities, subtract our deficiencies, and generate premises from the preceding elements that inductively and deductively serve our decision-making. We seem to have an immediate grasp of who we are, even though we make mistakes from time to time. This fact of our immediately grasping who we are testifies to the plausibility of the self being a trope.

## The self and strong supervenience

In Chapter III, I argued that the self should be understood as supervening *strongly* on the human being's physical and psychological properties. Post's type of 'determination' seems to be equivalent to what Kim calls the 'global' type of supervenience, and it is simply too ineffectual in accounting for the uniqueness that most of us attribute to the self. Strong supervenience in Kim's estimation implies necessary coextension between the supervenient properties and subvenient properties.[1] This is not a problem in itself, but it becomes a problem if coextension includes a reduction of the supervenient properties to the subvenient properties. I argued in the last pages of Chapter III that the concept of reduction, if interpreted a la Garfinkel, does not necessarily imply a *loss* of supervenient properties. The third major interpretation of supervenience, weak determination, is not robust enough to support the notion that the subvenient properties *determine* the supervenient properties. In weak supervenience, the same set of subvenient properties existing in two different worlds may give rise to two different sets of supervenient properties.[2] Therefore, no transworld identity for a given self would be guaranteed by weak supervenience. A conceivable difficulty for my theory of the self, given weak supervenience, would be the possibility of randomness entering the decision-making process. That is to say, when the person implicitly takes into consideration the present self relative to selecting an option for the future, there could be no assurance whatsoever that the projected future self has any connection at all to the present self. Of course, I am treating the future complex of projected self and future subvenient conditions as a world yet to be actualized. And, thus, transworld identity of the self is important to my thesis. Strong supervenience, in spite of its reductive tendencies, is preferable to either global supervenience or weak supervenience for purposes of the analysis of the self.

## Resemblance or identity? and trope or universal?

In Chapter IV, the brief historical glimpse of G. F. Stout's and D. C. Williams's contributions to the theory of abstract particulars (tropes) took us into the problem of identifying the appropriate concept underlying the reidentification of properties. Those who espouse universals as being the basis for the reidentification of properties choose identity as the primitive concept; those choosing tropes often appeal to resemblance instead. Panayot Butchvarov's defense of identity could not be ignored if one elects trope theory as an explication of the nature of the self. I will not recount the entire discussion engaged in above, but much turns on what one elects as the primitive concept in this discussion. If one elects identity as such, then it is natural to consider the relation of resemblance as being a universal. And for many philosophers this opens the door to an infinite regress. However, Butchvarov does not see it as being a vicious one in this case, and neither does Armstrong.[3] What is interesting here is that Armstrong suggests that any suggested tie between particular and property, whether class membership, instantiation, resemblance, etc., runs the risk of the infinite regress charge.[4] In any case, electing identity as the primitive concept leads to treating resemblance as being derivable from identity or as being interpreted in terms of identity. But could not identity be treated in terms of resemblance as the primitive concept? Those properties that are 'exactly similar' to one another could be described as being 'identical' to one another even though only the relation of resemblance truly holds here. This kind of linguistic 'looseness' is suggested by Williams in defense of resemblance as the primitive concept.

In Chapter IV I also defend the nature of the self as being a trope rather than being either a generic or specific universal. Whether treated as a generic universal or as a specific universal (the more likely of the two), the self would lose the uniqueness we normally attribute to it. Trope theory in application to the self would help preserve this characteristic. The self, as a trope and thus as a particular, is by definition unique because every particular is unique. Again, Butchvarov serves as the worthy proponent of an opposing point of view.

## The supervenient self and causal efficacy

The problem of how a supervenient property can have causal power is treated in Chapter V. This treatment, of necessity, had to refer to recent literature devoted to the body-mind problem. The reason I must deal with this problem in respect to my analysis of the self is due to the strong emphasis I place in Chapter VI and VII on the role of decision-making in the constitution of the self. Both Kathleen Lennon and Fred Dreske support the position that intentional states leading to intentional acts can be interpreted in terms of 'reasons' for behavior as well as in terms of physical causality. Both remain within the broadly defined camp of physicalism, and both attempt to find a causal role for reasons without simply giving up the distinction between causes and reasons in favor of an eliminative materialism. Lennon finds the concept of supervenience helpful in describing the mind's relationship to the physical. Dretske believes that intentional behavior can be understood in terms of the organism's instinct for survival.

## The self, temporality, and the community

In Chapters VI and VII, I consider an interpretation of the person's use of time as it pertains to the formation of the self. The person uses the self (most of the time implicitly) that has been formed on the basis of options exercised in the past to project him/herself into the future in a certain direction or mode. The self (as I use the term, it is similar to Sartre's transcendent ego [not transcendental ego] or Mead's 'me') is the temporal 'bridge' of the person's past into the future, and that is why I perceive the self interpreted in this fashion as the basis or source of personal identity. Even though this self is not static, it provides the proper picture of personal identity in that persons themselves are hardly static in their constitution. Thus, we must find that aspect of the person that is relatively stable through time in order to provide us with 'information' needed to make a reidentification of the person possible, and at the same time conforms to the dynamics of the person as not simply moving through time but using time. Thus, the self so interpreted is the proper focus for the reidentification of the person, rather than mere physical spatio-temporal continuity and psychological connectedness, although both of these feed into the self as subvenient properties.

Thus, in Chapters VI and VII I deal with the temporality of the person as it is shaped both by the social roles he/she must play and the moral decisions performed. I do not engage in an ontological analysis (understood in the analytic sense, not the Heideggerian) of time, i.e., whether time is best understood as tensed or as mere succession. The fact is: The existential approach used here simply 'sees' the person as using time in the tensed manner. In any case, these three chapters point up the necessity of treating the problem of personal identity in a far wider, more complex setting than the mere science fictional scenarios devised by Parfit. Decision-making, within the context of social roles and values, must also be considered.

## Consciousness is not the self

In Chapter VIII, I address the problem of circularity that some philosophers see as being involved in the notion of the self synthesizing the self. If we are consistent in our use of terminology, the problem is alleviated somewhat. Consciousness and the self (among other things) constitute the person, but consciousness and self are not identical functions of the person. If we interpret consciousness along the lines taken by Sartre, though there must be a 'fit' between the self (similar to the transcendent ego of Sartre) and consciousness, there is little or no circularity, because the Sartrean consciousness is a nihilating activity of the person. Its contents or intentional objects do not characterize it per se because in the next moment it may have a totally different set of contents. However, as was indicated in this chapter, if consciousness is treated on the Sartrean model, it does not have to be the case that consciousness of the 'Other' must always take the form of suspicion or opposition. Rather, Sartre's view of consciousness tempered with Mead's theme of cooperation between persons allows us to interpret the self, as does Ricoeur, from the moral point of view.

Further, consciousness should not be interpreted as the Kantian type of transcendental ego, i.e., as some kind of noumenal self standing behind those aspects of the person given within the phenomenal or experiential realm. Although Sartre has many objections to such an I, the following is particularly apt:

> Now, it is certain that phenomenology does not need to appeal to any such unifying and individualizing *I*. Indeed, consciousness is defined by intentionality. By intentionality consciousness transcends itself. It unifies itself by escaping from itself. [5]

Obviously, within the context of my theory of the self, consciousness must have powers beyond that of intentionality. It must also be that instrument by which the person surveys, reflects, judges, and chooses from those intentional objects that serve as the range of available options that play against the background of the self. The choice having been made, consciousness thereby commits the person to act in a certain manner which in turn provides more ubvenient material for the supervenient self.

## Thought experiments

Even though I indicate in Chapter IX that I believe that Parfit misuses thought experiments in respect to the problem of personal identity, there is a positive outcome to his work in this area: i.e., he forces us to place the problem in a wider context. There is no doubt that continuities in the physical and psychological dimensions of the person play a necessary role in the total process of how we are able to reidentify a person, whether ourselves or another. However, those 'continuities' are subsumed under the continuity of the self as described in this essay. Taken by themselves as attempts to resolve the problem of personal identity, they lead to conceptual frustration and/or the rejection of the concept of personal identity.

It may, in time, be the case that the concept of personal identity will be identified by the majority of us as being one of those beliefs belonging to 'folk psychology' and, therefore, translatable into a more acceptable scientific term or terms. But, until that time it would seem that it still serves a conceptual purpose in the areas of ascribing responsibility, determining moral rewards and sanctions, meting out legal sanctions, and making predictions regarding human behavior. Since these are serious concerns of humankind, it behooves us to be as clear as possible (given our present state of knowledge) about the basis on which personal identity is ascribed.

## Notes

Jaegwon Kim, *Supervenience and Mind* (Cambridge: Cambridge University Press, 1993), 71.
Ibid., 60ff.
D. M. Armstrong, *Universals: An Opinionated Introduction* (Boulder, CO: Westview Press, 1989), 54.
Ibid., 55.
Jean-Paul Sartre, *The Transcendence of the Ego*, 38.

# Bibliography

Aboulafia, Mitchell (1986), *The Mediating Self: Mead, Sartre, and Self-Determination.*, Yale University Press: New Haven.

Addis, Laird (1989), *Natural Signs: A Theory of Intentionality*, Temple University Press: Philadelphia.

Armstrong, D. M (1989), *A Combinatorial Theory of Possibility*, Cambridge University Press: Cambridge.

Armstrong, D. M. (1989), *Universals: An Opinionated Introduction*, Westview Press: Boulder, CO.

Baillie, James (1993), *Problems in Personal Identity*, Paragon House: New York.

Bechtel, William (1988), *Philosophy of Mind: An Overview for Cognitive Science*, Laurence Erlbaum Associates: Hillsdale, N.J.

Brockelman, Paul (1985), *Time and Self: Phenomenological Explorations*, The Crossroad Publishing Company: New York.

Butchvarov, Panayot (1979), *Being Qua Being: A Theory of Identity, Existence, and Predication*, Indiana University Press: Bloomington.

Butchvarov, Panayot (1979), 'Identity', in French, Peter (ed.), *Contemporary Perspectives in the Philosophy of Language*, University of Minnesota Press: Minneapolis.

Butchvarov, Panayot. (1988), 'Realism in Ethics', *Midwest Studies in Philosophy*, Vol. 12, pp. 395-412.

Butchvarov, Panayot, (1989) *Skepticism in Ethics*, Indiana University Press: Bloomington, Ind.

Campbell, Keith (1990), *Abstract Particulars*, Basil Blackwell: Oxford.

Campbell, Keith (1983), 'Abstract Particulars and the Philosophy of Mind', *Australasian Journal of Philosophy, Vol.* 61, June.

Cook, Gary A. (1993), *George Herbert Mead: The Making of a Social Pragmatist*, University of Illinois Press: Chicago.

Dennett, Daniel C. (1987), *The Intentional Stance..*: The MIT Press: Cambridge, Mass.

Dennett, Daniel C. (1991), *Consciousness Explained*, Little, Brown, and Company: Boston.

Dretske, Fred (1988), *Explaining Behavior*, The MIT Press: Cambridge, Mass.

Duerlinger, James (1993), 'Reductionist and Nonreductionist Theories of Persons in Indian Buddhist Philosophy', *Journal of Indian Philosophy*, Vol. 21, March.

Flanagan, Owen (1992), *Consciousness Reconsidered*, The MIT Press: Cambridge, Mass.

Garfinkel, Alan (1991), 'Reductionism.', in Boyd, Richard (ed.), *The Philosophy of Science*, The MIT Press: Cambridge, Mass.

Glover, Jonathan (1988), *I: The Philosophy and Psychology of Personal Identity*, Allen Lane-The Penguin Press: London.

Grimes, Thomas R. (1991), 'Supervenience, Determination, and Dependency.', *Philosophical Studies*, Vol. 62.

Hamlyn, D. W. (1984), *Metaphysics*, Cambridge University Press: Cambridge.

Heidegger, Martin (1988), *The Basic Problems of Phenomenology*, Indiana University Press: Bloomington.

Husserl, Edmund (1964), *The Phenomenology of Internal Time-Consciousness*, Indiana University Press: Bloomington.

Kim, Jaegwon (1979), 'Causality, Identity, and Supervenience in the Mind-Body Problem', *Midwest Studies in Philosophy*, Vol. 4.

Kim, Jaegwon (1982), 'Psychophysical Supervenience', *Philosophical Studies* Vol. 41.

Kim, Jaegwon (1983), 'Supervenience and Supervenient Causation', *Southern Journal of Philosophy* (Supplement), Vol.22.

Kim, Jaegwon (1984), 'Concepts of Supervenience', *Philosophy and Phenomenological Research*, Vol. 45, December.

Kim, Jaegwon (1984), 'Epiphenomenal and Supervenient Causation', *Midwest Studies in Philosophy*, Vol. 9.

Kim, Jaegwon (1987), '"Strong" and "Global" Supervenience Revisited', *Philosophy and Phenomenological Research*, Vol. 48, December.

Kim, Jaegwon (1990), 'Explanatory Exclusion and the Problem of Mental Causation', in Villaneuva, E. (ed.), *Information, Semantics, and Epistemology* Blackwell: Cambridge.

Kim, Jaegwon (1990), 'Supervenience as a Philosophical Concept', *Metaphilosophy*, Vol. 21, January/April.

Kim, Jaegwon (1993), *Supervenience and Mind*, CambridgeUniversity Press: Cambridge.

Kolak, Daniel and Martin, Raymond, (eds.), (1991), *Self and Identity*, Macmillan Publishing Company: New York.

Kolak, Daniel (1993), 'The Metaphysics and Metapsychology of Personal Identity', *American Philosophical Quarterly*, Vol. 30 January.

Lennon, Kathleen (1990), *Explaining Human Action*, Open Court: LaSalle, Ill.

Libet, Benjamin (1989), 'Neural Destiny: Does the Brain Have a Will of Its Own?' *The Sciences*, Vol. 29,March/April.

Locke, John (1975), *An Essay Concerning Human Understanding*, (ed.) Peter Nidditch, Clarendon Press: Oxford.

Mackie, Penelope (1987), 'Essence, Origin and Bare Identity', *Mind*, Vol. 96, April.

McInerny, Peter (1991), *Time and Experience*, Temple University Press: Philadelphia.

Mead, George H. (1934), *Mind, Self, and Society*, University of Chicago Press: Chicago.

Mead, George H. (1938), *The Philosophy of the Act*, (ed.) Charles W. Morris, University of Chicago Press: Chicago.

Miller, David L. (1973), *George H. Mead: Self, Language, and the World*, University of Texas Press: Austin, Texas.

Moore, G. E. (1984), 'Are the Characteristics of Particular Things Universal or Particular?' in Blackman, Larry (ed.), *Classics of Analytical Metaphysics*, University Press of America: Lanham, MD.

Nagel, Thomas (1986), *The View from Nowhere*, Oxford University Press: New York.

Natanson, Maurice (1956), *The Social Dynamics of George H. Mead*, Public Affairs Press: Washington, D.C.

Noonan, Harold W. (1989), *Personal Identity,*: Routledge: London.

Nozick, Robert (1981), *Philosophical Explanations*, Harvard University Press: Cambridge, Mass.

Papineau, David (1990), 'Why Supervenience?' *Analysis*, Vol. 50, March.

Parfit, Derek (1984), *Reasons and Persons*, Clarendon Press: Oxford.

Perry, John, (ed.),(1975), *Personal Identity*, U. of California Press: Berkeley.

Perry, John (1978), *A Dialogue on Personal Identity and Immortality*, Hackett Publishing Co.: Indianapolis.

Post, John (1987), *The Faces of Existence*, Cornell University Press.: Ithaca, N.Y.

Post, John (1991), *Metaphysics: A Contemporary Introduction*, Paragon House: New York.

Quine, W. V. (1987), *Quiddities*, Harvard University Press Cambridge, Mass..

Ricoeur, Paul (1991), 'Narrative Identity', in Wood, David (ed.), *On Paul Ricoeur*, Routledge: London.

Ricoeur, Paul (1992), *Oneself as Another*, University of Chicago Press: Chicago.

Rorty, Amelie Oksenberg,(ed.), (1976), *The Identities of Persons*, U. of California Press: Berkeley.

Sartre, Jean-Paul (1956), *Being and Nothingness,*: Philosophical Library: New York.

Sartre, Jean-Paul, (1990), *The Transcendence of the Ego*, Hill and Wang: New York

Schechtman, Marya (1990), 'Personhood and Personal Identity', *The Journal of Philosophy*, Vol. 87, February.

Searle, John (1992), *The Rediscovery of the Mind*, The MIT Press: Cambridge, Mass.

Shoemaker, Sydney (1963) *Self-Knowledge and Self-Identity*, Cornell University Press: Ithaca, N.Y.

Sorenson, Roy A. (1992), *Thought Experiments*, Oxford University Press: New York.

Stout, George F. (1936), 'Universals Again', *Proceedings of the Aristotelian Society* (Supplement), Vol. 15.

Stout, George F. (1984), 'The Nature of Universals and Propositions', in Blackman, Larry (ed.), *Classics of Analytical Metaphysics*, University Press of America: Lanham,MD.

Teller, Paul (1983), 'A Poor Man's Guide to Supervenience and Determination', *Southern Journal of Philosophy* (Supplement), Vol. 23.

Thomson, Judith Jarvis (1983), 'Parthood and Identity Across Time', *The Journal of Philosophy*, Vol. 80, April.

Tugendhat, Ernst (1986), *Self-Consciousness and Self-Determination*, The MIT Press: Cambridge, Mass.

Vesey, Godfrey (1974), *Personal Identity: A Philosophical Analysis*, Cornell University Press: Ithaca, N.Y.

Wilkes, Kathleen V. (1988), *Real People*, Clarendon: Oxford.

Williams, Donald C. (1966), 'The Elements of Being', Chapter VII of *Principles of Empirical Realism*, Charles Thomas, Publisher: Springfield, Ill.

Williams, Bernard (1973), *Problems of the Self*, Cambridge University Press: Cambridge.

Williams, Donald C. (1986) 'Universal and Existents', *Australasian Journal of Philosophy*, Vol. 64, March.

# Index